THE BBC MANUAL

TURNING YOUR BEDROOM INTO A BIBLE COLLEGE

GREGG JOHNSON

The BBC, Bedroom Bible College Manual
© Copyright held by MMI, Movement Makers International
P.O. Box 3940
Broken Arrow, OK 74013-3940
www.j12.com

International Standard Book Number 0-9766930-0-3

Design and layout by Personality™ (Los Angeles, California)

Printed in the United States of America. Fifth Printing March 2005

ACKNOWLEDGMENTS

We are all products of our environment. The kinds of people we allow into our circle of influence are the key to our success or failure as believers. For me, Grandpa had a large part in setting my life in the right direction. This manual has a lot to do with his influence in my life. Other people had a profound effect on me as well, helping me turn my bedroom into a Bible College. Thank you, Paul Furseth. Thank you, Mom.

As I write these words, I am aware that this is the second time around for writing acknowledgements for the BBC Manual. The first time was in 1993 when the phrase "Bedroom Bible College" was introduced at Summit '94 to over 10,000 Foursquare youth. Since that time, numerous young people, from across the nation and abroad, have shared testimonies with me of how their lives were positively changed by the challenge to turn their bedrooms into Bible Colleges. For this reason, I wanted to make sure a new generation of young people would be challenged to do the same.

Just yesterday, I received a phone call that Gary MacDonald went to be with the Lord. Gary was instrumental in the first edition of the BBC manual. He served as our National Youth Administrator for Summit '94. I dedicate this new edition of BBC in memory of Gary, a great pastor, husband, father, and friend.

TURNING YOUR
BEDROOM
INTO A BIBLE
COLLEGE

CONTENTS

INTRODUCTION

I think the seeds of desire for Godliness were planted early in my life through my grandfather. When I was about eight years old, he gave me a chart with a bunch of Scripture references on it, and told me that if I memorized the list of Scriptures he would buy me a bicycle. I never got the bicycle because I never learned all the verses. There were over 200 of them! But I did get the point. If I would hide God's Word in my heart and mind I would experience what the Bible calls "good success" (Joshua 1:8). My grandfather had a profound influence upon my life. His gentleness, joy and sense of peace were an anchor

to me. I can still see him sitting in the Lazy Boy chair sharing Jesus and a sense of destiny with me. He said I would be a man of God some day. His words and that chart helped move me in a God-direction. I'll never forget the morning my mother called me from my pup tent in the backyard. She sat me down in the living room to tell me my grandfather had passed away the night before. I cried and cried and cried. I couldn't go to his funeral because of the distance, but during that whole day of the funeral I sat at home in our own Lazy Boy chair with God's Word open, thinking about my grandfather and meditating on his favorite book — the Bible.

During this season of unquenchable desire for God's Word, I became what you might call a "Bible-junkie." I had to have more and more of the Word. This new-found desire came in stages. First, I found myself continually reminded that I even owned a Bible. Then, I gradually became more disciplined and aware of the Word's importance in my life. It wasn't long before my bedroom became a Bible College with Grandpa's chart on the wall and my desk covered in Bibles and books about the Bible. I became a student of the Word.

I am convinced that the single most important factor in my teenage years was the development of a consistent devotional life. Those times spent in the presence of Jesus on a regular basis provided the foundation to be transformed by Jesus, rather than be conformed to the world's system. Romans 12:2 tells us, *"Do not conform any longer to the pattern of this world, but be transformed by the renewing of your mind."* With a renewed mind that resulted from the discipline of a devotional life in the Word, God brought me through seven teenage years for which I will always be grateful and look back upon with joy.

During those years I learned the disciplines of **meditation** and **documentation**. In Psalm One, we have the portrait of a believer who loves God's law and meditates on it day and night. Those who love God's Word are like trees planted by the rivers of water. How's that for being "planted" in the right place? The Psalmist goes on to say that their leaves do not wither and whatever they do prospers. You can't beat those kinds of rewards. As a young teenager, I memorized and meditated upon such Scriptures. Because I had taken time to ponder the words and receive them into my spirit, I actually started to believe them. As a young teen, the development of my Christian convictions absolutely overshadowed the ungodly principles which contradicted God's desire for my life. When the Word of God enters your spirit, it becomes a cleansing agent that gives you power over sin (Psalm 119:11).

Along with a desire to spend time in God's presence, came the corresponding desire to write down what I was learning in my walk with Him. In those early years, I can remember writing out pages and pages of Scripture, documenting truths that emerged as I meditated on the Word. No one had told me to do this. I did it because I wanted to! For me, writing down truths and insights given by the One with whom I had become close, was an appropriate response. I marked up a few manuals and diaries during this time in my life — marked them with exclamation points, insights and revelation that I had received during meditation on the greatest book ever written!

This **Bedroom Bible College** Manual that you hold in your hand will help you develop a healthy devotional life. I challenge you to become a "Bible-junkie," the kind of person who can't live without the Word! I challenge you to take on the disciplines found in this manual. Mark up this manual! Use it as a personal diary. Give God one year of determined devotion and I believe you will give Him the next one after that. It will become a lifestyle, a way of living.

THE BIBLE - WHAT A BOOK!

I was in the 7th grade at the time. It was a Sunday afternoon and my family and I were on our way home from church. As we were heading up 124th Street, I saw one of my friends from school walking along the sidewalk with a black leather-bound book in his hand. I was pumped. I couldn't wait to get to school the next day to talk to my friend about the book he had been carrying. To my utter surprise he denied the whole

thing. He told me he wasn't on 124th Street the previous day. Bottom line — he didn't want his other friends to know he attended church or even owned a Bible! What is it about the Bible that creates such a stir and such a fear among so many, even among those who believe? The answer is fairly obvious. It's a book about God and the plan of salvation — an unpopular subject in a fallen

world. Another reason for the reaction is ignorance. Most people aren't aware of how genius the Bible really is — a fact admitted even by those who don't believe in God or what the Bible says.

THE BIBLE - THE MOST INFLUENTIAL BOOK EVER WRITTEN

No other book has influenced such a wide array of great men as the Bible. Christopher Columbus is noted as saying, "It was the Lord who put into my mind to sail from here to the Indies. There is no question that the inspiration was from the Holy Spirit because he comforted me with rays of marvelous illumination from the Holy Scriptures…"[1]

Abraham Lincoln said, "I believe the Bible is the best gift God has ever given to man. All the good from the Savior of the world is communicated to us through this book."

George Washington said, "It is impossible to rightly govern the world without God and the Bible."

Napoleon said, "The Bible is no mere book, but a Living Creature with a power that conquers all that oppose it."

Daniel Webster said, "If there is anything in my thoughts or style to commend, the credit is due to my parents for instilling in me an early love for the Scriptures."

W.E. Gladstone said, "I have known ninety-five of the world's great men in my time and of these eighty-seven were followers of the Bible."[2]

Even agnostics and atheists admit to the influence of the Bible upon mankind. Goethe, the famous German poet and antagonist of Christianity said, "The human mind, no matter how far it may advance in every other department, will never transcend the height and moral culture of Christianity as it is shown in Gospels."[3]

Immanuel Kant, the famous German philosopher and not a Christian in the slightest sense said, "The existence of the Bible, as a book for people, is the greatest benefit which the human race has ever experienced. Every attempt to belittle it is a crime against humanity."[4]

The words of Jesus recorded in the Bible are the most influential words ever spoken. Jesus, a few days before He was crucified said, "Heaven and earth will pass away, but my words will not pass away" (Luke 21:33). This prediction by Jesus a few days before his death would seem highly improbable, after all, He wasn't as well known at that time as your run-of-the-mill music recording artist is today. Yet as G.F. MacLean has observed, "Never did it seem more improbable that it (Jesus' prediction) should be fulfilled. But, as we look across the centuries, we see how it has been realized. His words have passed into the law, they have passed into doctrine, they have passed into proverbs, they have passed into consolations, they have never passed away. What human teacher ever dared to claim an eternity for his words."[5]

Bernard Ramm said, "Statistically speaking the Gospels are the greatest literature ever written. They are read by more people, quoted by more authors, translated into more tongues, represented in more art, set to more music that any other book or books written by any man in any century in any land. But the words of Christ are not great on the grounds that they have such statistical edge over anybody else's words. They are read more, quoted more and translated more because they are the greatest words ever spoken."[6]

THE BIBLE IS A MIRACULOUS COMPILATION

The Bible was written over 1,600 years, by over 40 different authors from very different walks of life, on three different continents, during times of war and peace, in three different languages: Hebrew, Aramaic (a small portion of the Old Testament) and Greek. These facts make the Bible an impossible book to write… if man had written it. The hands of men recorded it but the mind of God wrote it through those hands. There is a unity of thought that cannot be mistaken. We can begin at Genesis and read through to the end. "There is no jar. We can pass from one style of literature to another as easily as though we were reading a story written by one hand and produced by one life, and indeed we have here a story produced by one mind (2 Peter 1:21) though not written by one hand."[7]

THE BIBLE AND HISTORICAL ACCURACY

The Bible is the most historically accurate piece of literature in the world. Josh McDowell says, "The Bible, compared with other ancient writing, has more manuscript evidence than ten pieces of classical literature combined."[8]

The reliability of the Old Testament is understood when one discovers that the Jews preserved the Old Testament like no other piece of literature has ever been preserved. Men (scribes, lawyers and Masoretes) were trained in special classes to learn how to make sure every letter, syllable, word and paragraph was kept in the original form. No other writing has been protected from error so zealously. Concerning the New Testament, the same is true. The New Testament, which has been in existence for over 18 centuries, contains no texts that are in serious dispute among scholars today. In fact, there are less questions about the reliability of the New Testament manuscripts than the writings of Shakespeare which were written by one playwright, less than 400 years ago. The Bible truly is supernatural in its historical reliability.

THE BIBLE AND PERSECUTION

No other book has been persecuted and ridiculed more than the Bible. Yet no book has been as victorious over its persecutors as the Bible. "Voltaire, the noted French infidel who died in 1778, said that, in one hundred years from this time Christianity would be swept away from existence and passed into history. But what has happened? Voltaire has passed into history; while the circulation of the Bible continues to grow in almost all parts of the world carrying blessing everywhere it goes."[9] Fifty years after Voltaire's death, the Geneva Bible Society used his press and house to produce stacks of Bibles. What an irony!

John Lennon of the Beatles was quoted as saying "Christianity will go. It will vanish and shrink. I need not argue about that. I'm right and I will be proved right. We're more popular than Jesus Christ right now."[10] Just a few years after these words were spoken the Beatles broke up and in 1980, John Lennon was dead.

The Bible has been able to withstand all of the criticism and skepticism hurled in its direction. "Infidels, with all their assaults, make about as much impression on this book as a man with a jack hammer would on the pyramids of Egypt. When the French monarch proposed the persecution of the Christians in his dominion, an old statesman and warrior said to him, 'Sire, the church of God is an anvil that has worn out many hammers.' So the hammers of infidels have been pecking away at this book for ages, but hammers are worn out and the anvil still endures. If this book had not been the Word of God, man would have destroyed it long ago. Emperors and popes, kings and priests, princes and rulers have all tried their hand at it; however, they die and the book still lives."[11]

The Bible stands alone in its conception, its influence, its distribution, its accuracy and in its universal appeal. "Kings and princes have studied it. It has fascinated lawyers and doctors, astronomers and housewives, farmers and physicists. A never-ending stream of humanity has been born, married, and buried under the sound of Bible reading. It has become the book of the Eskimo and the African, the giant Watusi and the tiny pygmies. No other book has such universal appeal to all men of all temperaments, all races, all employments, all social standing, all economic means, and all gifts of intelligence."[12]

No book has had such an influence on the human race as the Bible. It is the foundation upon which our society stands. You can't teach history without the Bible. "It is impossible to teach history fairly and fully without a frank recognition of the influence of the Bible. Study the Reformation, the Puritan Movement, the Pilgrim journeys, the whole of early American history. We can leave the Bible out only by trifling with the facts."[13]

The Bible's influence on literature is staggering. Many educators argue that an understanding of the Bible is essential for the proper understanding of English literature. Dr. McAfee says, "Take any of the great books of literature and black-out the phrases which manifestly come directly from the English Bible...you would mark them beyond recovery."[14]

The Bible's influence on law is far reaching. Can you imagine what it would be like to live in a country where the Ten Commandments were not observed? The founding documents of our country are based upon the Bible. The laws of our land find their foundation in the laws of the Bible.

The Bible's influence has extended into all areas of life including politics, philosophy, the arts and music. Take the Bible out of any of these areas of discipline and influence and you have drastically altered the landscape of human life and history.

The Bible - there is no other book like it and there will never be another book like it. It is God's Book to man.

THE BIBLE GOD'S LOVE LETTER TO MAN

I'll never forget the scene, I had just gotten up to speak to a group of young people at Camp Whispering Oaks in Central Texas. There was a young lady on the front row who wasn't listening to a word I was saying. Now, it's not the most encouraging sign when you want to get through to a group of

young people, to have those closest to you preoccupied. She was writing. I decided I wanted to know if what she was writing down was more interesting than what I was saying. After having wrestled the note from her (to her horrification) I proceeded to read the letter to the whole group. You may already have an idea what the letter said. Oh, you don't know the name but you probably already know the line. Well the name was Josh and you guessed it - the line was "I love Josh...I love Josh...I love Josh." That's all the letter said but it meant a lot to this young teenager. Puppy love is real to puppies. By the way, I think it took Josh a couple of years to forgive me for the incident. He was the most embarrassed.

Have you ever received a "love letter"? They are amazing pieces of literature, aren't they? Love letters are written with a specific someone in mind. They are best understood in the context of relationship. I'm reminded of the story of a university professor who stood before his class and began to ridicule the Bible. Throwing the Bible on his desk top, and pounding on its cover he proceeded to let his students know how offended he was that such an inaccurate (in his view) piece of literature could influence so many. One of the students responded to his outrage by asking him if he was truly offended by the Bible, to which the professor replied, "Yes I am!" continuing his verbal attack. The student responded by saying, "Sir, that's what you get for reading someone else's mail." The Bible wasn't primarily written for unbelievers. It was written for believers and those who are open to the truth. The Bible isn't first and foremost a book to be cerebrally studied as a text book but to be read as a letter - a "love letter" from God to man. Notice I said "first and foremost." The Bible can withstand the closest scrutiny of the mind; yet, if that is all you bring to it, you will miss the heart and spirit of the Word altogether.

"Love letters" are wonderful things. They don't have to be long to keep you mesmerized for hours. How many times have you read the same "love letter" over and over and over again — studying every word, lingering over every thought, catching every inflection.

You can't read a true "love letter" without reading between the lines. When you read between the lines, you are moving beyond what is being "said" to what is also being "meant." What did he or she mean by that comment? Words sometimes can't convey what the heart wants to say. When it comes to the Bible, the Holy Spirit helps us with what's between the lines.

Understanding what's between the lines is the result of being in relationship with the author of the letter. The Bible's author is God. Because God has chosen to use people in His plan, He chose to use men to write His letters. The Lord is gracious. Not only does He use us, He allows us to be us when He uses us. That's why different books of the Bible reflect the personalities of those who wrote them. For God to be glorified doesn't require the annihilation of the human personality. After all, the Bible tells us that we are made in His image. This doesn't mean that the Lord will use just anybody. The Bible says that *holy* men of God spoke as they were carried along by the Holy Spirit (2 Peter 1:21). In order to be used by God you need to be "set apart." That's what "holy" means — to be "set apart" for a special purpose.

I've received a few love letters in my life. Not only have I read them over and over again, reading between the lines, enjoying my relationship with the sender, but I've also enjoyed the "scent" if you know what I mean. That special smell didn't come from the paper mill, but from a bottle of perfume. The letter had the fragrance of that scent. That "scent" is the presence of the Holy Spirit. There is "someone" on the Word of God and that "someone" is Him.

When you read your Bible devotionally and even when you study it, remember that it was written with you in mind. God was thinking of you when He wrote the Bible, the Bible He wrote through the hands of men, because God loves using people in His plan!

THE BIBLE ~ A LIBRARY BETWEEN THE COVERS

The Bible is without question the most unique book ever written. First of all, it was written by God through the hands of over forty different men. Secondly, it contains 66 books within its covers written over a period of approximately 1,600 years. And thirdly, it is the most persecuted book in the history of mankind yet the greatest seller of all time. These few reasons and many more set the Bible apart from all other books. Getting an overview of the Bible will be helpful on your journey through the Word.

- The word "Bible" comes from the Greek word "biblos" which means book.
- The Bible is God's written revelation of His will for man.
- The Bible is divided into two major divisions: the Old Testament and the New Testament. The word "testament" means covenant or agreement.
- The Old Testament is God's covenant concerning the *law*. The New Testament is God's covenant concerning *grace,* which came through Jesus Christ.
- The Old Testament begins with God (Genesis 1:1). The New Testament begins with Jesus Christ (Matthew 1:1).
- The Old Testament *looks forward* to Jesus. The New Testament *looks back* to Jesus, with the cross in the middle.

TURNING YOUR BEDROOM INTO A BIBLE COLLEGE

The Bible is truly an amazing book both in its unity and diversity. Even though it was written over a period of 1,600 years on three different continents (Asia, Africa, and Europe), by over 40 different authors including kings, princes, philosophers, poets, prophets, shepherds and fishermen, it contains a supernatural unity. It covers hundreds of topics including sin, salvation, racism, women's rights, human rights, heaven, hell, etc. In it, you will find unity and agreement, the kind of unity and agreement that you would be hard pressed to find between two authors living at the same time. Just think of it, most of these authors never knew each other, having lived in various cultures during different points in history. Many didn't have a clue that the others were or would be writing. Yet there is an undeniable unity found within and between the writings. Impossible, unless someone was putting it all together supernaturally. It only makes sense that a supernatural God would produce a supernatural book.

Understanding the Bible as a whole will come easier after you gain an understanding of its parts. The most basic division within the Bible is the division between the Old and New Testaments. The Old Testament is divided into 39 books while the New Testament is divided into 27 books.

UNDERSTANDING THE BIBLE AS A WHOLE WILL COME EASIER AFTER YOU GAIN AN UNDERSTANDING OF ITS PARTS.

THE BIBLE AT A GLANCE

Take time to study this page to familiarize yourself with an overview of the Bible's structure and divisions. Doing this will help you to find sections of Scripture quicker and easier. This works well when your pastor asks the congregation to turn to a certain place in the Bible. You'll probably be the first one there! It won't get you to heaven, but it will relieve some of the frustration and even embarrassment down here on earth!

+5 LAW (5 BOOKS)
Purpose: To help the nation of Israel function as a sane society (civil laws), and to function as a holy society (moral laws).

+12 HISTORY (12 BOOKS)
Purpose: To record the events of mankind (especially Israel), revealing God's hand on the affairs of man.

+5 POETRY (5 BOOKS)
Purpose: To express emotions, to share wisdom for living.

+17 PROPHECY (17 BOOKS - 5 MAJOR/12 MINOR PROPHETS)
Purpose: To record the results of obedience and disobedience towards God, given through the mouth of God's prophets and priests.

+4 GOSPELS (4 BOOKS)
Purpose: To give an accurate account of the life of Christ: His birth, death, resurrection, life-style and teachings.

+1 ACTS (1 BOOK)
Purpose: To record the birth and expansion of the earthly church.

+21 EPISTLES (21 BOOKS)
Purpose: To give believers instruction concerning life and living.

+1 REVELATION (1 BOOK)
Purpose: To give a foretelling of the end, and its hope for believers.

An effective way to remember the basic sections of the Bible would be to take the number of books in each type of literature and memorize the order. Create a rhythm as you say them. This will help you memorize them much quicker.

$$5...12...5.5.12....4...1...21.1$$

To help you remember the different kinds of literature, take the first letter of each literature type, and memorize the letters in order.

L H P P G A E R

Again, create a rhythm or tune to help you remember. Committing both of these sequences to memory will give you an internal quick reference of the structure of the Bible. *Five minutes a day for seven days and you'll never forget it.*

THE OLD TESTAMENT

The first five books of the Bible are called the Pentateuch or the Five Books of Moses (Genesis - Deuteronomy). These five books include an account of the beginning of the world and the history of the nation of Israel that would become the channel for the Messiah. The Pentateuch records the ups and downs of this nation, what happened when they obeyed God and what happened when they didn't. Much can be learned about God and the life of faith from these first five books of the Bible (1 Corinthians 10:1-13).

The Historical Books include those from Joshua to Esther. These record the key events in the history of the nation of Israel: their conquest over the land of Canaan (Joshua), the establishment of the nation which ended up divided (1 & 2 Samuel - 2 Chronicles), and their captivity and return from captivity (Ezra - Esther).

The next five books, Job - Song of Solomon, are called the Books of Poetry or Wisdom. In them you will learn how to worship (the Psalms are the hymnal of the Bible), how to live (Proverbs), what is vanity (Ecclesiastes), why the godly suffer (Job), and about love between a husband and wife reflecting God's love between Him and His people (Song of Solomon).

The next 17 books (Isaiah - Malachi) are the Prophetical Books which outline the rise and fall of the people of God. The prophets were God's mouthpiece to the nation of Israel calling them back to a relationship with Him. The prophets cover a period of 500 years, beginning at the time of Samuel when the kingdoms were divided into Judah and Israel. Both of these kingdoms, Israel the northern kingdom of ten tribes, and Judah, the southern kingdom of two tribes, fell into captivity because of their turning from God. Israel fell first to the Assyrians. Judah fell approximately 130 years later to the Babylonians. Some Old Testament prophets spoke before the captivities, some during and some afterwards.

Prophets were not popular people because they were only raised up by God when His people were "off track." Therefore, they came to confront sin in kings and common man alike. The Old Testament prophets were bold men who didn't compromise and were often killed for their stance. The prophets spoke directly to people about their immediate sin and they also spoke about future events. In the ministry of the prophets, we can find many insights and principles that span the ages. In other words, we can learn much from the prophets of the Old Testament even today.

It is interesting to note that none of the Old Testament prophets ever spoke of the Church, even though they prophesied the coming of the Messiah. Jesus Himself announced that He was going to build His church (Matthew 16:18). The church was the mystery kept hidden before this point (Ephesians 3:3-10).

THE NEW TESTAMENT

Between the New and Old Testaments, there was a period of 400 years called the "silent years" — a time in history when God didn't speak through His prophets. Then came the promise fulfilled — Jesus the Messiah was born.

The first four books of the New Testament are called the Gospels. The word "gospel" is derived from two words: "God" meaning *good* and "spell" meaning *tidings*. So the gospel means "good tidings" or "good news." Each of the four gospels presents the good news of Jesus' birth, life, death and resurrection. You may wonder why there are four different accounts of Jesus instead of just one. Each of the gospels presents a different aspect of the life and person of Christ:

- In Matthew He is portrayed as the *King*, written with the Jews in mind.
- In Mark He is portrayed as the *Servant*, written with the Romans in mind.
- In Luke He is portrayed as the *Son of Man*, written with the Greeks in mind.
- In John He is portrayed as the *Son of God*, with believers in mind.

Viewing Christ from four different angles is much like viewing a statue from four different sides — without the angles you will not see the complete picture. The gospels give us a full view of the different aspects of Jesus.

The Book of Acts is the one historical book of the New Testament. Acts records the beginning of the church and the spread of the Gospel. In the Gospel of Luke, we have what Jesus *began* to do while on earth. In the Book of Acts we have what He *continued* to do by the Holy Spirit. Christ's ascension to heaven is the closing scene in Luke. In Acts it is the opening event (Luke 24:49-51 and Acts 1:10-11). The Book of Acts records the acts of the Holy Spirit through the apostles and the church. The "Holy Spirit" is mentioned about 70 times. The word "witness" is mentioned over 30 times.

The next division in the New Testament is the Epistles or letters. Thirteen of the twenty-one epistles were written by Paul. He wrote nine of them to specific individuals (1 Timothy - Philemon). Each of these epistles was written as a letter for a specific purpose. These letters are valuable instructions in Christian "day to day" living. While the Gospels tell us "who to believe in," the Epistles tell us "how to live." The general epistles (James - Jude) were also written for a specific need or group of people. They cover truths that are needed by Christians of every age.

The last book in the library of the Word is the Book of Revelation. It is the revelation of Jesus Christ and His ultimate eternal victory over Satan. In it, a new heaven and a new earth are established with the saints of God ruling and reigning with Christ forever. It is the only book that especially promises blessing to those who read it. Maybe this is because, in it, Satan's final doom is outlined more than in any other book, along with the fact that, whenever we focus on Jesus revealed we are, of all people, most blessed.

This is the library between the covers of the greatest Book ever written. It is the only Book that is able to make you wise for salvation (2 Timothy 3:15).

FEED... LEARNING TO OBSERVE

Feeding on the Bible is the greatest meal you will ever sit down to enjoy. Jeremiah said, *"Your words were found and I ate them. And your word was to me the joy and rejoicing of my heart"* (Jeremiah 15:16a NKJV).

Learning the principles of observation will transform God's Word from a "soup and sandwich" special into a smorgasbord of delights. The only catch, you'll have to pay more for the smorgasbord than you do for the "soup and sandwich" special. You get what you pay for. As the old saying goes, "There are no free lunches!"

In order to "pay the price," you'll need to "review the rewards" over in your heart and mind. The benefits of Bible reading and study are supernatural. In other words, there is something about getting into "The Word" that produces unexplainable positive results in your life. There is something "on" the Bible that isn't "on" any other book. That "something" is the breath of God. His Word is living, it's active, and it's sharper than a razor blade (Hebrews 4:12).

Check out seven of the many benefits that come from "The Word."

THE BIBLE GIVES LIGHT - PSALM 119:105

"Your word is a lamp to my feet and a light to my path"

Everyday, you make hundreds of choices: some big, some small, some far reaching, some of little consequence. As you fill your heart with the Word of God you will develop an inner flashlight, a built-in compass that will point you in the right direction. Your sensitivity to the terrain around you will be heightened. As a "lamp to your feet" the Word will help you with the *next step*. As a "light to your path" it will help you with your *basic direction*. The word will help you now and it will help you later. The Word of God is a light.

THE BIBLE PRODUCES PEACE - JOHN 16:33A (NKJV)

"These things I have spoken to you, that in Me you may have peace..."

There are two kinds of peace, peace *from* the storm and peace *in* the storm. The peace God offers is the kind of peace that isn't dependent upon easy circumstances. Between the words "spoken" and "peace" are the words "in Me." The Bible produces peace for those who are "in Him." How could Paul the Apostle write a book about joy (Philippians) from the chains of a prison cell? Paul was "in Christ" more than he was "in jail."

THE BIBLE BRINGS JOY - JOHN 15:11

"I have told you this so that my joy may be in you and that your joy may be complete."

"My joy" and "your joy" — double joy, what a deal! As we read the Bible, we receive the joy of Jesus and our own joy as well. In a materialistic society, it's good to know that the joy that God gives doesn't come from what we *own* but from what we *hear* — God's words bring double joy.

THE BIBLE PROVIDES CLEANSING - JOHN 15:3

"You are already clean because of the word I have spoken to you."

Our lives can be likened to bucket filled with holes — as we fill the bucket of our lives with the "water of the Word," the strain cleanses us. Barry McGuire, a pioneer of contemporary Christian music, was once accused of being brainwashed because he was a Christian. Barry responded, "Hey, at least my brain is clean." The Bible is a powerful cleanser of the mind and spirit.

THE BIBLE OFFERS THE ASSURANCE OF SALVATION - 1 JOHN 5:13

*"I write these things to you who believe in the name of the Son of God
so that you may know that you have eternal life."*

Feelings come and go. Emotions can be misleading. Our emotional state can actually be affected by a chemical imbalance, not to mention the weather. There are those who seem to struggle with the assurance of their salvation more than others. A commitment to Bible reading and study will bring you confidence and assurance of salvation. We are also promised that the Spirit of God will bear witness with our spirits that we are children of God (Romans 8:16). Two great confidence builders: the "Word" and the "witness" of the Spirit.

THE BIBLE GIVES WISDOM - PSALM 119:99

"I have more insight than all my teachers, for I meditate on your statutes."

Wisdom, insight, understanding — these are for those who get into the Word. Jesus, at the age of twelve, had insight and understanding that caused the teachers in the temple to sit and listen to Him in amazement. This sense of understanding that Jesus had didn't come by being God (He gave up His rights as God), but by being a student of the Word. You can grow in wisdom and understanding beyond your years, also. Make the Word of God your meditation. Your teachers will notice the difference.

THE BIBLE BRINGS GOOD SUCCESS - JOSHUA 1:8 (NKJV)

"This Book of the Law shall not depart from your mouth, but you shall meditate in it day and night, that you may observe to do according to all that is written in it. For then you will make your way prosperous and then you will have good success."

Show me someone who is committed to meditation in the Word of God and I will show you someone who is successful. You can't get away from it; blessing follows those who follow God. The natural mind wants to "pick a fight" with this kind of promise, yet the spiritual mind receives it with joy. Remember though, the *promise* is connected to the *prerequisite* - meditate.

FEELINGS COME AND GO. EMOTIONS CAN BE MISLEADING.

HOW TO READ THE BIBLE DEVOTIONALLY

The Bible is no easy book to read. The numerous translations available, along with the structure of the Bible (66 books within one), not to mention the cultural context in which it was written, make it a hard book on which to get a handle. Yet, with a truckload of desire (this is God's part, Philippians 2:13) and a pile of discipline (this is our part) we can get a "grip" on the Word.

READ DAILY

"Anybody can do almost anything for a little while." The gold medal goes to the person who through perseverance wins the prize. Someone has said, "By perseverance the snail reached the ark." There is no substitute for daily consistency. Establishing a pattern of daily Bible reading will build into

your life character traits of steadfastness and faithfulness. Paul talked about the importance of "pattern" in Philippians 3:17, "Join with others in following my example, brothers, and take note of those who live according to the *pattern we gave you*" (italics added). The word *pattern* speaks of repetition, consistency and re-occurrence. When a criminal is brought to trial, their past record is often a key factor in the outcome of their trial. If you were on trial for being a Bible reader would there be enough evidence to convict you? Daily Bible reading is the foundation for a healthy devotional life. When I was 16 years old I made a covenant with the Lord that I would spend at least 5 minutes a day reading the Bible for the rest of my life. Decades later, I could probably count on my fingers and toes how many days I've missed! This daily discipline has been an anchor over the years.

Throughout the years I have gone through stages. At the age of 14, I began the pattern of spending two hours a day right after school, Monday through Friday, in my bedroom reading, praying and meditating on the Word. When I went to high school, my schedule changed so dramatically that the "*pattern*" had to change. Yet, I continued to read the Word often after classes at the school before I went to work as a busboy at the Red Carpet Steak House. I was committed. If I didn't spend a certain amount of time (i.e. 30 minutes) in the Word it bothered me big time! I believe those early years of determined Bible reading set a foundation for the rest of my life.

The story is told of a famous violinist who was asked how many hours she practiced each day. To everyone's surprise she said that she didn't practice as much as she did when she was a teenager. She then went on to say that when she was younger, she practiced eight hours a day. She said it formed a foundation that didn't need to be laid again. To read the Word daily during your early years (or from this moment on), will form a foundation that can not be taken away from you. Proverbs tells us, "Train up a child in the way he should go and when he is old he will not turn from it." Learning the scales early will allow you to "ad lib" later on without missing a beat or losing the tune. Determine to read daily — even if you think it will kill you — it won't. It will build in you a sense of accomplishment, self-respect and healthy rhythm. Like someone once said, "Why do we give our bodies three square meals a day and our spirits one cold snack a week?" Feed on the Word daily and you will receive the rewards.

READ DELIGHTFULLY

"Attitude determines altitude." We should come to the Bible with a humble heart and a positive mind. We need to come happy even if we feel lousy. We need to come submitted even if we feel like we have a "bone to pick" with God. We need to come broken and open even though we would rather come crushed, closed, and mad about it.

We need to come into the Word like we come into His presence — with thanksgiving. If you come to the Word with a humble heart, God will lift you up. David serves as a great example of how to come to God and His Word. David often came to God when he was down, but he often left "up." Check out the first and last verse of each of the following Psalms: 13, 55, 57, 59, 60, and 61. Spending time with God and His Word will change your perspective. Much of what we go through is nothing more than "mind over matter." Once we get God's mind on the issue, lots of things just don't seem to matter. Submit to joy even though it's easier sometimes to submit to pessimism.

When you come to the Word, come believing. The Bible has some pretty amazing things to say, things that unless God said them, would seem absolutely outlandish. Statements like, "Lose your life and you'll find it" or "give and it will be given to you" or "accept one another then just as Christ has accepted you." These claims, predictions and commands go against the grain of fallen man. We don't like revelation. Our minds reel in disbelief. Yet what the Bible says is true. Come believing and the devil won't be able to do his deceiving.

When you come to the Word, come receiving. It is very easy to slip into the "what can I get to give" routine. Some people only come to the Word in order to "get" something to "give" to someone else. For those in "full-time ministry," it is tempting to use devotional reading as an opportunity to only prepare sermons. Come to "get" something for yourself and you will end up "giving" out of the abundance of your own "getting." The best way to touch someone else is out of the overflow of your own well.

When you come to the Word, come perceiving. The Bible is a gold mine, but the gold isn't found on the surface. Psalm 119:18 says, *"Open my eyes so I may see wonderful things in your law."* This is not a reference to poor eyesight. It expresses something we have all experienced, the ability to not see what is right in front of us. We must come to the Word with an inner ear and eye. We need to come to the Word asking, "Why did the author say what he said? What are the implications of what he is saying to me?" As someone so aptly put it, "Come to the Bible with *self exposure* in mind."

In order to "perceive" the Word you must be willing to read slowly and repeatedly. One quick chapter a day might "keep the devil away," but for reasons other than you might suppose. Reading yet never *believing, receiving* or *perceiving* is what will make the devil happy.

PRACTICAL POINTERS FOR CONSISTENT BIBLE READING

1. CHOOSE A SPECIFIC TIME.

For many, the most practical time of day to have their quiet time is first thing in the morning. To begin the day with devotions means that daily distractions end up coming too late — your time with God has already taken place. Setting aside time in the morning also sets the tone for the whole day. If you are a night person the evening may be your best time. The only challenge is that at night distractions can often get the best of you. A certain minister decided early in his life that he would live by following the rule, "No Bible, no breakfast." For me, it has been, "No Bible, no bed." I will not go to sleep at night without having spent some time in the Word of God. So, whether it be "No Bible, no breakfast" or 'No Bible, no bed," make sure that you commit yourself to a daily time.

2. CHOOSE A SPECIFIC PLACE.

When I started my devotional life at 14, my bedroom became a Bible College. I had my Scripture chart on the wall and my desk was covered with different Bible translations and helpful study books, along with my notebook. Now, my briefcase has become my Bible College. I often have my devotions on airplanes or in hotel rooms because of my extensive travel schedule. Most people (especially young people) have a much less traveled life-style. **Turn your bedroom into a Bible College.** Do it now and you will never regret it.

3. CHOOSE A SPECIFIC AMOUNT OF TIME.

The journey of 1,000 miles begins with the first step. I would suggest committing yourself to five or ten minutes a day for one month. Even though this manual is designed to help you meet the goal of giving one year of concentrated effort to developing a strong devotional life, approaching your commitment to it in one-month segments may help you meet the challenge. At the end of your one-month commitment choose to commit another month staying at your set amount of time or moving up 15 minutes a day. Spending 15 minutes a day reading the Word devotionally will put you in the "league of the few" who actually accomplish such a goal. In all of this, we need to remember that the goal isn't to "get through the Bible" but to allow the Bible to "get through to us." If we are not careful we will end up worshiping the *goal* instead of *God*.

4. CHOOSE A SPECIFIC READING SCHEDULE.

Opening up the Bible and starting to read wherever your eye falls won't do a lot for your spiritual growth. A humorous story is told of a person who asked God for guidance and opened his Bible to read the account of Judas, who after he had betrayed the Lord, went out and hung himself. Obviously that wasn't good guidance so he flipped to another section of scripture that read, "Go and do thou likewise." Choosing a specific reading schedule will save you from receiving guidance that is out of context.

As a teenager I read through the entire Bible at least three times. If you have never fully read *through the Bible* from cover to cover, I challenge you to do this next year. Granted, some parts of the Bible are more interesting and personally practical than other sections. Reading through the ceremonial laws found in Leviticus or genealogies found in Matthew won't give you insight into how to respond to your brothers and sisters stealing your sweater; yet, the hard work of wading through the material will produce a life-style of discipline. By reading just three to four chapters each day you will have read through the entire Bible in one year. The **Read Through the Bible in One Year** chart found on pages **30-33** can be used to record your progress. I have found this system of Bible reading to be a great foundation for Bible study. As a teenager I used my **Read Through the Bible in One Year** chart as a launching pad for further study and meditation. Don't get locked into a "works program" though. If you get behind, try to catch up. If you can't seem to get through your three to four chapters a day, work on one or two. Remember the goal isn't to "get through the Bible" but to allow the Bible to "get through to you." The other chart, **An Overview of the Bible in One Year** found on pages **34** and **35** will help you read 365 key chapters of the Bible in one year. Maybe you could begin with the **An Overview of the Bible in One Year** and then go for the **Read Through the Bible in One Year** plan the following year. I have found that I function best with boundaries. Give me a specific reading schedule and I'll follow it. Give me an open Bible and I'll haphazardly slip from place to place. Many have also found it very beneficial to read through the Psalms and the Proverbs within a month. Five Psalms and one Proverb a day will get the job done. This is a great way to keep you "built up" through the Psalms and "wisened up" in the Proverbs.

5. CHOOSE TO KEEP A DIARY.

Disciples are documenters. The three most practical words in the English language (or any language) could be "write it down."

As a teenager, I knew I had the "Bible bug" when I started writing out what I was reading in the Word. I'll never forget those years of daily documentation. I would read my allotted section of Scripture and then write it out in paraphrase (to paraphrase is to write out in your own words what you have just read). My life is scattered with different diaries that I have kept over the years.

Why not begin a spiritual diary? **Why not use this manual as your spiritual diary for now?** "Mess up" this manual! I have a manual similar to this that I "messed up" (documented my thoughts and insights from the Word) when I was a teenager. I still have it today. Commit yourself to one of the challenges on the next page!

THE DEVOTIONAL CHALLENGE

There are three challenges in the **BBC** Manual: the **Devotional** Challenge, the **Meditation** Challenge and the **Double** Challenge. The Devotional Challenge (#1 or #2) will require between 5 to 15 minutes per day of Bible reading. (The reading schedule is based upon the **chronological order** of events found in the Bible).

CHALLENGE #1

Read three to four chapters of the Bible each day using the **Read Through the Bible in One Year** chart. You will have read every verse and chapter of the Bible within one year.

CHALLENGE #2

Read one key chapter from the Bible each day using the **Overview of the Bible in One Year** chart. You will read 365 chapters that will give you a good grasp of what the Bible says from Genesis to Revelation.

CHALLENGE # 1 - READ THROUGH THE BIBLE IN ONE YEAR

JANUARY

- [ ] 1/ Genesis 1,2
- [ ] 2/ Genesis 3-5
- [ ] 3/ Genesis 6-9
- [ ] 4/ Genesis 10, 11
- [ ] 5/ Genesis 12-15
- [ ] 6/ Genesis 16-19
- [ ] 7/ Genesis 20-22
- [ ] 8/ Genesis 23-26
- [ ] 9/ Genesis 27-29
- [ ] 10/ Genesis 30-32
- [ ] 11/ Genesis 33-36
- [ ] 12/ Genesis 37-39
- [ ] 13/ Genesis 40-42
- [ ] 14/ Genesis 43-46
- [ ] 15/ Genesis 47-50
- [ ] 16/ Job 1-4
- [ ] 17/ Job 5-7
- [ ] 18/ Job 8-10
- [ ] 19/ Job 11-13
- [ ] 20/ Job 14-17
- [ ] 21/ Job 18-20
- [ ] 22/ Job 21-24
- [ ] 23/ Job 25-27
- [ ] 24/ Job 28-31
- [ ] 25/ Job 32-34
- [ ] 26/ Job 35-37
- [ ] 27/ Job 38-42
- [ ] 28/ Exodus 1-4
- [ ] 29/ Exodus 5-7
- [ ] 30/ Exodus 8-10
- [ ] 31/ Exodus 11-13

FEBRUARY

- [ ] 1/ Exodus 14-17
- [ ] 2/ Exodus 18-20
- [ ] 3/ Exodus 21-24
- [ ] 4/ Exodus 25-27
- [ ] 5/ Exodus 28-31
- [ ] 6/ Exodus 32-34
- [ ] 7/ Exodus 35-37
- [ ] 8/ Exodus 38-40
- [ ] 9/ Leviticus 1-4
- [ ] 10/ Leviticus 5-7
- [ ] 11/ Leviticus 8-10
- [ ] 12/ Leviticus 11-13
- [ ] 13/ Leviticus 14-16
- [ ] 14/ Leviticus 17-19
- [ ] 15/ Leviticus 20-23
- [ ] 16/ Leviticus 24-27
- [ ] 17/ Numbers 1-3
- [ ] 18/ Numbers 4-6
- [ ] 19/ Numbers 7-10
- [ ] 20/ Numbers 11-14
- [ ] 21/ Numbers 15-17
- [ ] 22/ Numbers 18-20
- [ ] 23/ Numbers 21-24
- [ ] 24/ Numbers 25-27
- [ ] 25/ Numbers 28-30
- [ ] 26/ Numbers 31-33
- [ ] 27/ Numbers 34-36
- [ ] 28/ Deuteronomy 1-3

MARCH

- [ ] 1/ Deuteronomy 4-6
- [ ] 2/ Deuteronomy 7-9
- [ ] 3/ Deuteronomy 10-12
- [ ] 4/ Deuteronomy 13-16
- [ ] 5/ Deuteronomy 17-19
- [ ] 6/ Deuteronomy 20-22
- [ ] 7/ Deuteronomy 23-25
- [ ] 8/ Deuteronomy 26-28
- [ ] 9/ Deuteronomy 29-31
- [ ] 10/ Deuteronomy 32-34
- [ ] 11/ Joshua 1-3
- [ ] 12/ Joshua 4-6
- [ ] 13/ Joshua 7-9
- [ ] 14/ Joshua 10-12
- [ ] 15/ Joshua 13-15
- [ ] 16/ Joshua 16-18
- [ ] 17/ Joshua 19-21
- [ ] 18/ Joshua 22-24
- [ ] 19/ Judges 1-4
- [ ] 20/ Judges 5-8
- [ ] 21/ Judges 9-12
- [ ] 22/ Judges 13-15
- [ ] 23/ Judges 16-18
- [ ] 24/ Judges 19-21
- [ ] 25/ Ruth 1-4
- [ ] 26/ 1 Samuel 1-3
- [ ] 27/ 1 Samuel 4-7
- [ ] 28/ 1 Samuel 8-10
- [ ] 29/ 1 Samuel 11-13
- [ ] 30/ 1 Samuel 14-16
- [ ] 31/ 1 Samuel 17-20

APRIL

- 1/ 1 Samuel 21-24
- 2/ 1 Samuel 25-28
- 3/ 1 Samuel 29-31
- 4/ 2 Samuel 1-4
- 5/ 2 Samuel 5-8
- 6/ 2 Samuel 9-12
- 7/ 2 Samuel 13-15
- 8/ 2 Samuel 16-18
- 9/ 2 Samuel 19-21
- 10/ 2 Samuel 22-24
- 11/ Psalms 1-3
- 12/ Psalms 4-6
- 13/ Psalms 7-9
- 14/ Psalms 10-12
- 15/ Psalms 13-15
- 16/ Psalms 16-18
- 17/ Psalms 19-21
- 18/ Psalms 22-24
- 19/ Psalms 25-27
- 20/ Psalms 28-30
- 21/ Psalms 31-33
- 22/ Psalms 34-36
- 23/ Psalms 37-39
- 24/ Psalms 40-42
- 25/ Psalms 43-45
- 26/ Psalms 46-48
- 27/ Psalms 49-51
- 28/ Psalms 52-54
- 29/ Psalms 55-57
- 30/ Psalms 58-60

MAY

- 1/ Psalms 61-63
- 2/ Psalms 64-66
- 3/ Psalms 67-69
- 4/ Psalms 70-72
- 5/ Psalms 73-75
- 6/ Psalms 76-78
- 7/ Psalms 79-81
- 8/ Psalms 82-84
- 9/ Psalms 85-87
- 10/ Psalms 88-90
- 11/ Psalms 91-93
- 12/ Psalms 94-96
- 13/ Psalms 97-99
- 14/ Psalms 100-102
- 15/ Psalms 103-105
- 16/ Psalms 106-108
- 17/ Psalms 109-111
- 18/ Psalms 112-114
- 19/ Psalms 115-118
- 20/ Psalms 119
- 21/ Psalms 120-123
- 22/ Psalms 124-126
- 23/ Psalms 127-129
- 24/ Psalms 130-132
- 25/ Psalms 133-135
- 26/ Psalms 136-138
- 27/ Psalms 139-141
- 28/ Psalms 142-144
- 29/ Psalms 145-147
- 30/ Psalms 148-150
- 31/ 1 Kings 1-4

JUNE

- 1/ Proverbs 1-3
- 2/ Proverbs 4-7
- 3 /Proverbs 8-11
- 4/ Proverbs 12-14
- 5/ Proverbs 14-18
- 6/ Proverbs 19-21
- 7/ Proverbs 22-24
- 8/ Proverbs 25-28
- 9/ Proverbs 29-31
- 10/ Ecclesiastes 1-3
- 11/ Ecclesiastes 4-6
- 12/ Ecclesiastes 7-9
- 13/ Ecclesiastes 10-12
- 14/ Song of… 1-4
- 15/ Song of… 5-8
- 16/ 1 Kings 5-7
- 17/ 1 Kings 8-10
- 18/ 1 Kings 11-13
- 19/ 1 Kings 14-16
- 20/ 1 Kings 17-19
- 21/ 1 Kings 20-22
- 22/ 2 Kings 1-3
- 23/ 2 Kings 4-6
- 24/ 2 Kings 7-10
- 25/ 2 Kings 11-14:20
- 26/ Joel 1-3
- 27/ 2 Kings 14:21-25; Jonah 1-4
- 28/ 2 Kings 14:26-29; Amos 1-3
- 29/ Amos 4-6
- 30/ Amos 7-9

JULY

- 1/ 2 Kings 15-17
- 2/ Hosea 1-4
- 3/ Hosea 5-7
- 4/ Hosea 8-10
- 5/ Hosea 11-14
- 6/ 2 Kings 18, 19
- 7/ Isaiah 1-3
- 8/ Isaiah 4-6
- 9/ Isaiah 7-9
- 10/ Isaiah 10-12
- 11/ Isaiah 13-15
- 12/ Isaiah 16-18
- 13/ Isaiah 19-21
- 14/ Isaiah 22-24
- 15/ Isaiah 25-27
- 16/ Isaiah 28-30
- 17/ Isaiah 31-33
- 18/ Isaiah 34-36
- 19/ Isaiah 37-39
- 20/ Isaiah 40-42
- 21/ Isaiah 43-45
- 22/ Isaiah 46-48
- 23/ Isaiah 49-51
- 24/ Isaiah 52-54
- 25/ Isaiah 55-57
- 26/ Isaiah 58-60
- 27/ Isaiah 61-63
- 28/ Isaiah 64-66
- 29/ Micah 1-4
- 30/ Micah 5-7
- 31/ Nahum 1-3

AUGUST

- 1/ 2 Kings 20, 21
- 2/ Zephaniah 1-3
- 3/ Habakkuk 1-3
- 4/ 2 Kings 22-25
- 5/ Obadiah, Jeremiah 1, 2
- 6/ Jeremiah 3-5
- 7/ Jeremiah 6-8
- 8/ Jeremiah 9-12
- 9/ Jeremiah 13-16
- 10/ Jeremiah 17-20
- 11/ Jeremiah 21-23
- 12/ Jeremiah 24-26
- 13/ Jeremiah 27-29
- 14/ Jeremiah 30-32
- 15/ Jeremiah 33-36
- 16/ Jeremiah 37-39
- 17/ Jeremiah 40-42
- 18/ Jeremiah 43-46
- 19/ Jeremiah 47-49
- 20/ Jeremiah 50-52
- 21/ Lamentations 1-5
- 22/ 1 Chronicles 1-3
- 23/ 1 Chronicles 4-6
- 24/ 1 Chronicles 7-9
- 25/ 1 Chronicles 10-13
- 26/ 1 Chronicles 14-16
- 27/ 1 Chronicles 17-19
- 28/ 1 Chronicles 20-23
- 29/ 1 Chronicles 24-26
- 30/ 1 Chronicles 27-29
- 31/ 2 Chronicles 1-3

SEPTEMBER

- 1/ 2 Chronicles 4-6
- 2/ 2 Chronicles 7-9
- 3/ 2 Chronicles 10-13
- 4/ 2 Chronicles 14-16
- 5/ 2 Chronicles 17-19
- 6/ 2 Chronicles 20-22
- 7/ 2 Chronicles 23-25
- 8/ 2 Chronicles 26-29
- 9/ 2 Chronicles 30-32
- 10/ 2 Chronicles 33-36
- 11/ Ezekiel 1-3
- 12/ Ezekiel 4-7
- 13/ Ezekiel 8-11
- 14/ Ezekiel 12-14
- 15/ Ezekiel 15-18
- 16/ Ezekiel 19-21
- 17/ Ezekiel 22-24
- 18/ Ezekiel 25-27
- 19/ Ezekiel 28-30
- 20/ Ezekiel 31-33
- 21/ Ezekiel 34-36
- 22/ Ezekiel 37-39
- 23/ Ezekiel 40-42
- 24/ Ezekiel 43-45
- 25/ Ezekiel 46-48
- 26/ Daniel 1-3
- 27/ Daniel 4-6
- 28/ Daniel 7-9
- 29/ Daniel 10-12
- 30/ Esther 1-3

OCTOBER

- 1/ Esther 4-7
- 2/ Esther 8-10
- 3/ Ezra 1-4
- 4/ Haggai 1-3; Zechariah 1,2
- 5/ Zechariah 3-6
- 6/ Zechariah 7-10
- 7/ Zechariah 11-14
- 8/ Ezra 5-7
- 9/ Ezra 8-10
- 10/ Nehemiah 1-3
- 11/ Nehemiah 4-6
- 12/ Nehemiah 7-9
- 13/ Nehemiah 10-13
- 14/ Malachi 1-4
- 15/ Matthew 1-4
- 16/ Matthew 5-7
- 17/ Matthew 8-11
- 18/ Matthew 12-15
- 19/ Matthew 16-19
- 20/ Matthew 20-22
- 21/ Matthew 23-25
- 22/ Matthew 26-28
- 23/ Mark 1-3
- 24/ Mark 2-6
- 25/ Mark 7-10
- 26/ Mark 11-13
- 27/ Mark 14-16
- 28/ Luke 1-3
- 29/ Luke 4-6
- 30/ Luke 7-9
- 31/ Luke 10-13

NOVEMBER

- 1/ Luke 14-17
- 2/ Luke 18-21
- 3/ Luke 22-24
- 4/ John 1-3
- 5/ John 4-6
- 6/ John 7-10
- 7/ John 11-13
- 8/ John 14-17
- 9/ John 18-21
- 10/ Acts 1,2
- 11/ Acts 3-5
- 12/ Acts 6-9
- 13/ Acts 10-12
- 14/ Acts 13, 14
- 15/ James 1,2
- 16/ James 3-5
- 17/ Galatians 1-3
- 18/ Galatians 4-6
- 19/ Acts 15-18:11
- 20/ 1 Thessalonians 1-5
- 21/ 2 Thessalonians 1-3; Acts 18:12-19:10
- 22/ 1 Corinthians 1-4
- 23/ 1 Corinthians 5-8
- 24/ 1 Corinthians 9-12
- 25/ 1 Corinthians 13-16
- 26/ Acts 19:11-20:1; 2 Corinthians 1-3
- 27/ 2 Corinthians 4-6
- 28/ 2 Corinthians 7-9
- 29/ 2 Corinthians 10-13
- 30/ Acts 20:2; Romans 1-4

DECEMBER

- 1/ Romans 5-8
- 2/ Romans 9-11
- 3/ Romans 12-16
- 4/ Acts 20:3-22
- 5/ Acts 23-25
- 6/ Acts 26-28
- 7/ Ephesians 1-3
- 8/ Ephesians 4-6
- 9/ Philippians 1-4
- 10/ Colossians 1-4
- 11/ Hebrews 1-4
- 12/ Hebrews 5-7
- 13/ Hebrews 8-10
- 14/ Hebrews 11-13
- 15/ Philemon; 1 Peter 1,2
- 16/ 1 Peter 3-5
- 17/ 2 Peter 1-3
- 18/ 1 Timothy 1-3
- 19/ 1 Timothy 4-6
- 20/ Titus 1-3
- 21/ 2 Timothy 1-4
- 22/ 1 John 1, 2
- 23/ 1 John 3-5
- 24/ 2 John, 3 John, Jude
- 25/ Revelation 1-3
- 26/ Revelation 4-6
- 27/ Revelation 7-9
- 28/ Revelation 10-12
- 29/ Revelation 13-15
- 30/ Revelation 16-18
- 31/ Revelation 19-22

AN OVERVIEW OF THE BIBLE IN ONE YEAR

GENESIS 1❑ 2❑ 3❑ 4❑ 5❑ 6❑ 7❑ 8❑ 9❑ 10❑ 11❑ 12❑ 13❑ 14❑

33❑ 35❑ 37❑ 39❑ 40❑ 41❑ 42❑ 43❑ 44❑ 45❑ 46❑ 47❑

15❑ 16❑ 17❑ 18❑ 19❑ 20❑ 26❑ 32❑ 33❑ 34❑ **LEVITICUS** 26❑

DEUTERONOMY 1❑ 2❑ 4❑ 5❑ 6❑ 7❑ 8❑ 10❑ 11❑ 20❑ 28❑ 29❑

11❑ 12❑ 13❑ 14❑ 15❑ 23❑ 24❑ **JUDGES** 1❑ 2❑ 3❑ 6❑ 7❑ 8❑

9❑ 10❑ 11❑ 12❑ 13❑ 14❑ 16❑ 17❑ 18❑ 19❑ 20❑ 21❑ 22❑ 23❑

1 KINGS 1❑ 2❑ 3❑ 8❑ 9❑ 10❑ 13❑ 17❑ 18❑ 19❑ **2 KINGS** 2❑

17❑ **2 CHRONICLES** 1❑ 7❑ 20❑ 30❑ 32❑ **EZRA** 3❑

PSALMS 1❑ 2❑ 5❑ 19❑ 23❑ 27❑ 34❑ 51❑ 61❑ 63❑ 84❑ 103❑

ECCLESIASTES 3❑ **SONG OF SOLOMON** 2❑ **ISAIAH** 6❑ 25❑

EZEKIEL 1❑ 2❑ 3❑ 37❑ **DANIEL** 1❑ 3❑ 5❑ 6❑ **HOSEA** 11❑

NAHUM 1❑ **HABAKKUK** 1❑ **ZEPHANIAH** 2❑ **HAGGAI** 1❑

26❑ 27❑ 28❑ **MARK** 1❑ 2❑ 3❑ 4❑ 5❑ 6❑ 7❑ 8❑ 9❑ 10❑ 11❑

21❑ 24❑ **JOHN** 1❑ 2❑ 3❑ 4❑ 5❑ 6❑ 7❑ 8❑ 9❑ 10❑ 11❑ 12❑

11❑ 16❑ 17❑ 26❑ 27❑ 28❑ **ROMANS** 3❑ 7❑ 8❑ 12❑ 13❑ 14❑

GALATIANS 3❑ 4❑ 5❑ **EPHESIANS** 1❑ 2❑ 3❑ 4❑ 5❑ 6❑

1 THESSALONIANS 3❑ **2 THESSALONIANS** 2❑ **1 TIMOTHY** 1❑ 4❑

HEBREWS 2❑ 11❑ 12 **JAMES** 1❑ 5❑ **1 PETER** 1❑ 4❑ **2 PETER** 1❑

5❑ 16❑ 17❑ 18❑ 19❑ 20❑ 21❑ 22❑ 23❑ 24❑ 25❑ 26❑ 27❑ 28❑ 32❑

XODUS 1❑ 2❑ 3❑ 4❑ 5❑ 6❑ 7❑ 8❑ 9❑ 10❑ 11❑ 12❑ 13❑ 14❑

UMBERS 10❑ 11❑ 12❑ 13❑ 14❑ 16❑ 17❑ 33❑ 34❑

0❑ 31❑ 32❑ 33❑ **JOSHUA** 1❑ 2❑ 3❑ 4❑ 5❑ 6❑ 7❑ 8❑ 9❑ 10❑

3❑ 14❑ 15❑ 16❑ **RUTH** ❑ **1 SAMUEL** 1❑ 2❑ 3❑ 4❑ 5❑ 6❑ 8❑

4❑ 31❑ **2 SAMUEL** 2❑ 6❑ 7❑ 8❑ 11❑ 12❑ 13❑ 22❑

❑ 4❑ 5❑ 6❑ 17❑ 22❑ **1 CHRONICLES** 1❑ 12❑ 13❑ 14❑ 15❑ 16❑

NEHEMIAH 1❑ 2❑ 3❑ 8❑ **ESTHER** 4❑ **JOB** 1❑ 2❑ 38❑ 42❑

39❑ 150❑ **PROVERBS** 1❑ 3❑ 7❑ 9❑ 10❑ 22❑ 31❑

0❑ 53❑ 55❑ **JEREMIAH** 2❑ 15❑ 31❑ 38❑ **LAMENTATIONS** 3❑

OEL 2❑ **AMOS** 4❑ **OBADIAH** ❑ **JONAH** 3❑ 4❑ **MICAH** 6❑

ECHARIAH 14❑ **MALACHI** 3❑ **MATTHEW** 5❑ 6❑ 13❑ 14❑ 21❑

2❑ 13❑ 14❑ 15❑ 16❑ **LUKE** 1❑ 2❑ 3❑ 4❑ 9❑ 10❑ 15❑ 16❑ 18❑

3❑ 14❑ 15❑ 16❑ 17❑ 18❑ 19❑ 20❑ 21❑ **ACTS** 1❑ 2❑ 5❑ 9❑ 10❑

CORINTHIANS 12❑ ❑13 14❑ 15❑ **2 CORINTHIANS** 4❑ 12

PHILIPPIANS 1❑ 2❑ 3❑ 4❑ **COLOSSIANS** 1❑ 3❑

TIMOTHY 1❑ 3❑ 4❑ **TITUS** 2❑ 3❑ 4❑ **PHILEMON** ❑

JOHN 3❑ **2 JOHN** ❑ **3 JOHN** ❑ **JUDE** ❑ **REVELATION** 1❑ 2❑ 3❑ 12❑

HOW TO STUDY THE BIBLE

Turning your bedroom into a Bible College will require more than a "hit and miss" approach to Bible reading and study. Along with a basic devotional reading of the Bible, you can develop the skills

that will help you study the Bible. Serious Bible students know they must separate *devotional reading* from *Bible study*. Yet, at the same time, as you develop basic observational skills, *devotional reading* can actually become *devotional Bible study*. Even though the challenge of the **BBC** Manual is a challenge for Bible reading and Bible meditation, the Bible study approaches offered in this chapter will greatly benefit those who want to develop a strong devotional life along with those who want to delve into deeper Bible study.

DIFFERENT KINDS OF BIBLE STUDY

The Bible is a book comprised of 66 different books written by over 40 different authors over a period of 1,600 years. (You've read this before, haven't you? Repetition with variety is the key to learning.) Different kinds of literature are found within the pages of the Bible. The Bible is much like a magazine, composed of a collection of several different kinds of writing: news stories, editorials, comics, advertisements, etc. Different kinds of literature are also found in the pages of the Bible: historical, poetical, prophetic, narrative, etc. Because of the many different books, along with the different kinds of literature found in the Bible, you can study it many different ways. Four of them are listed below:

BOOK STUDY - As has already been mentioned, the Bible is composed of 66 different books, 39 are found in the Old Testament and 27 are found in the New Testament. A book study is self explanatory. It means that you focus on one specific book of the Bible and study what that particular book has to say.

WORD STUDY - A word study involves choosing a specific word (i.e. love) and learning about where that word is used in the Bible, how many times it is used and what the word means in the original language or languages.

CHARACTER STUDY - The Bible is filled with all kinds of people — many of them worth the time and effort required to study their lives. (There are approximately 2,930 men and women mentioned in the Bible.) Lots of insight into right living (and even wrong living) can be found through the lives of many people within the Word.

TOPICAL STUDY - The Bible is a book of many topics. You may want to do a study on "the grace of God" or "the blood of Jesus" or "the early Church." A topical study and a word study are often closely related.

Book studies, word studies, character studies and topical studies all add up to Bible study. Reading the Bible *devotionally* and studying the Bible analytically are two different disciplines, but they both spell growth.

DIFFERENT KINDS OF BIBLE TOOLS

In order to get the most out of your study you will need some tools. Just as a carpenter needs a hammer, saw, nails and a level, so the Bible student needs a Bible and a few good books about the Bible to get the job done. Many people make one of the two following mistakes. Some will only read the Bible. Others will read every other book except the Bible. Both extremes are unhealthy. The following four tools will be sufficient for a basic study of God's Word.

1. A GOOD STUDY BIBLE. There are many good study Bibles on the market today. These Bibles provide background information on the different books of the Bible. Some of them provide definitions for key Hebrew and Greek words. In my opinion, one of the most enjoyable and productive activities in Bible study has been the study of cross references. Cross references are verses of Scripture that touch on the same subject I am studying. Many study Bibles such as the *Spirit Filled Life Bible*, the *Thompson Chain Reference Bible* and the *NIV Study Bible* have this feature on every page. Another great study Bible for young people is the *Student Bible* published by Zondervan.

2. **A BIBLE CONCORDANCE.** An invaluable tool for looking up where certain words are used throughout the Bible. Most study Bibles contain an abbreviated concordance near the end. An exhaustive concordance lists all of the occurrences of every word in the Bible (i.e. *Strong's Exhaustive Concordance).* A *complete* concordance will list all the occurrences of major words, a *compact or handy concordance* will list key references on selected words.

3. **A BIBLE DICTIONARY.** Another handy tool for the Bible student is a good Bible Dictionary. Frequently, you will come across certain words, places, subjects or doctrines that will need to be explained more fully. A Bible Dictionary will provide you with the information you cannot find when only reading the Bible. The *Eerdman's Bible Dictionary* or *Vine's Complete Expository Dictionary of the Old and New Testament Words* are good choices.

4. **A ONE-VOLUME COMMENTARY.** Because the Bible was written in a different time, in a culture different than our own, to a people quite different than ourselves, it is often necessary to draw on the insights of Bible scholars to explain hard to understand sections. A good, one-volume commentary is the *Eerdman's Bible Commentary.* Even though the comments are generally brief there is great value in having one book at your disposal that expands on any section of Scripture that you may be reading. A great tool for me over the years has been *Wuest's Word Studies in the Greek New Testament.* This three-volume set offers the Bible student, with no understanding of the Greek language, easy to understand insights in the meaning of key words and the cultural context in which they were used.

Why not invest in these tools? Begin with a good study Bible. You may also want to purchase a few less expensive Bibles or go online so that you can compare different translations and paraphrases. The *New King James Version,* the *New International Version,* the *New American Standard Version* and the *Living Bible* paraphrase are excellent choices. *The Message: The Bible in Contemporary Language* has become a favorite for many young people.

All of the above resources can be viewed and/or purchased *through the internet.* A Google™ search (**google.com**) is all that stands between you and the information you want. Here is a list of some great websites to get you started: **CrossWalk.com, StudyLight.com, Bible.org.** These websites contain many different helpful tools. For instance, *Strong's Concordance* can be found on **CrossWalk.com.** Instead of going out and purchasing it in book form, you can get it online. An explanation of how to use *Strong's Concordance* and *Vines Expository Dictionary* in book form is explained on page 52-54.

LEARNING TO SEE WHAT YOU ARE READING

Many of us read, but we don't see. In other words we don't pay attention to details. Have you ever read a whole page of a book and had no idea what you just read? Learning to be an observer is the foundation to effective reading and study. Observation is a skill that doesn't come without a mental workout. Yet, with the development of any skill, determination and dedication end up producing delight. Nothing is more exciting than the joy of personal discovery. Unearthing treasures in the Bible for yourself produces an inner desire to search for more.

As a basic rule, be looking for three things when reading the Bible: **KEY WORDS, PROMISES** and **COMMANDS.** You may want to use a different color to highlight each of these when you discover them through observation. Also, while observing, look for *contrasts* and *comparisons, illustrations, repetitive phrases or words, questions* and *"cause and effect"* relationships. I have found that being on the lookout for "cause and effect" relationships has made the Bible a much more practical book for living. For instance, I discovered the recipe for power over sin by looking for "cause and effect" relationships while reading the Psalms. David said, "Your word have I hid in my heart so I might not sin against you." *The cause* — hide God's Word in your heart. *The effect* — a new power over sin. Always be looking for "cause and effect," the "if you do this, then that will happen" kind of verses. As you develop your powers of observation you will enjoy your Bible study much more.

BOOK STUDY

STUDY SHEETS FOR THE FOLLOWING TOPICS CAN BE FOUND AT THE BACK OF THE MANUAL. CHECK OUT THE EXAMPLES IN THIS CHAPTER.

The most natural divisions found within the Bible are 66 divisions which make up the 66 different books of the Bible. Each book was written to a specific group of people, church or person for a specific reason. Some books of the Bible are long (i.e. Isaiah with 66 chapters), others are short (i.e. Jude with one chapter). Some are more difficult to understand than others (i.e. the book of Revelation versus the Gospel of John). In beginning a book study, it would be advisable to select a shorter book (four to six chapters) that has a practical theme (i.e. Ephesians and Philippians).

In order to get an overall grasp of the book it would be best to read it over and over again until you feel the book begin to fall into place. This may mean reading the book over 10 to 15 times. I have found it helpful to ask a few questions before I start these repeated readings.

- Who wrote the book?
- To whom was it written?
- What was the purpose of the book?

By answering these three questions at the beginning, it gives me a foundation for observation. This is not unlike reading the prologue of a book in order to get a quick overview of the contents. These three questions are easily answered in the few pages devoted to an overview of the Bible book found just before that particular book in almost every study Bible available today. After you have read the specific book you have chosen to study you are ready to use the "BOOK STUDY" sheet.

CHAPTER STUDY

Chapter study is one of the most natural ways to approach the Bible. Most chapters contain a single theme or message over a span of 20-30 verses. Chapter study is much like a book study, the difference being in the amount of material being observed. Use the "CHAPTER STUDY" sheet to help you record your observations.

VERSE STUDY

Verse study is another way to approach the Bible. Certain verses of the Bible have been an anchor for the souls of many. For instance, John 3:16, the most quoted verse in the Bible, has been used to bring multiplied millions into the Kingdom. In a verse study you are able to focus on just a few words, examining the structure and determining the message. Take advantage of the "VERSE STUDY" sheet provided.

WORD STUDY

The Bible wasn't written in the English language. The Old Testament was mostly written in the Hebrew language while the New Testament was written in Greek. Because of this, many key words in the Bible have meaning that cannot be fully understood without studying them in their original language. For the average Bible reader, the following three questions will give you what you are looking for when unearthing the meaning of a particular word.

How many times is the word used in the Bible? In order to answer this question you will need to use an exhaustive concordance of the Bible. *Strong's Exhaustive Concordance* is the most popular. An example of how to use *Strong's Concordance* is offered on pages 53-54. Some words appear so often in the Bible (i.e. heaven) that it may not be possible to look up every reference. In such cases, reading the few words around each key word in *Strong's Concordance* will give you its context or usage in that verse. From here you can determine which references will be most applicable to your study. By looking up your key word in *Strong's Concordance* you will be able to find out how many times the word is used in the Bible, both the Old and New Testaments.

What is the root meaning? You don't have to be a Hebrew or Greek scholar to find out the root meaning of key words. With all of the study helps available today all you need to understand is the English language. *Strong's Concordance* will give you the root meaning of every Hebrew and Greek word in the Bible. At the end of each reference you will find a number that corresponds with the same number at the back of the concordance under "Hebrew and Chaldee Dictionary," or "Greek Dictionary of the New Testament." A good Bible dictionary will also provide the root meaning for most key words in the Bible. An example of how to use a Bible dictionary is found on pages 53-54.

How is the word used? It should be noted that the definitions for words in *Strong's Concordance* are literal definitions and don't necessarily give the accurate meaning of the word. The root meaning of a word tells you of its origin but how the word is used is the primary determining factor in its meaning. The meaning of a word can be discovered by:

● Finding out where it is first used in the Bible.
● Finding out where it is used the most.
● Reading it in its context.

Studying key words will open up key sections of Scripture with new meaning and depth

CHARACTER STUDY

Some of the most colorful and interesting people who have ever lived are found in the Bible. People like Adam, Moses, Joseph, David, Solomon, the three Hebrew children, Samson, Mary, John the Baptist, Peter and Paul are platformed on the pages of biblical history. First Corinthians 10:11 tells us that their deeds were recorded for our profit. In order to profit from their example you'll need to study their lives. The "CHARACTER STUDY" sheet will help you record your observations. An example is provided.

TOPICAL STUDY

A topical study allows you to focus on one specific subject in order to understand God's mind on that subject. One of the ways we know the Bible to be the Word of God is in its consistency. This becomes obvious in topical study. From Genesis to Revelation you will find a unity of thought on any topic in the Bible because the Bible doesn't contradict itself. The Bible was obviously inspired by one God, even though written by many hands, over a period of many years. A good concordance is the key to effective topical study. To begin a topical study, use your concordance to help you locate all the references related to your topic. If you were to do a study on the "blood of Christ" or the "will of God" you would look up all references under the words "blood" or "will." Use the "TOPICAL STUDY" chart to record your observations. A study on the will of God is shown on page 47. When I looked up the word "will" in Strong's Concordance I found over 3,000 references. For this reason, I went to the abbreviated concordance in the back of my Bible on the "will of God." From the Scriptures I studied, I discovered that God's will is not as hard to understand as I thought it would be!

SUGGESTED TOPICS TO STUDY

SALVATION,   THE BLOOD OF JESUS,
THE WILL OF GOD,
THE TABERNACLE,
THE SERMON ON THE MOUNT,
THE TEN COMMANDMENTS, HOLINESS,
THE FRUIT OF THE SPIRIT,
THE GIFTS OF THE SPIRIT,
THE HOLY SPIRIT, BLESSING,
WITNESSING, LOVE, FAITH,
PEACE, HEAVEN, HELL, FEAR, ANGELS

BOOK STUDY

NAME OF BOOK: I John
DATE:

WHO IS THE AUTHOR? John the Apostle
TO WHOM WAS IT WRITTEN? christians in ephesus

WHEN WAS IT WRITTEN? about 90 A.D.
WHERE WAS IT WRITTEN? probably Ephesus

WHY WAS THIS BOOK WRITTEN? (DISCOURAGEMENT, CONFLICT, TENSION, ETC) John wrote this letter to give assurance to those who believed that Jesus came in the flesh. A heresy had arisen stating that Jesus didn't really come in the flesh. That matter was essentially evil & spirit was good. John wrote to combat this heresy.

WHAT IS THE MAIN THEME?
- Jesus is the son of God come in the flesh.
- Believers must live like Jesus we can know what we know!

1:4; 1:9; 2:3; 4:2; 4:20
2:1; 3:23; 5:13

KEY VERSE(S)?
- Know- gin osko (39 x's) obtained not by mere intellectual activity, but by the holy spirit
- Love- Agape - essential nature of God
- Fellowship- Koinonia- communion
- Life - Zoe -God's life, eternal life

COMMANDS?
- Do not love the world (2:15)
- See that what you have heard from the beginning remains in you. (2:24)
- Abide in Him (2:28)
- let us love in deed & in truth (3:18)

PROMISES?
- If we confess our sins he is faithful & just to forgive us. (1:9)
- Greater is He who is in you. (4:4)

PRINCIPLES (CAUSE AND EFFECT)
- No one who is born of God will continue to sin because God's seed remains in him. (3:9a)
- we love Him because He first loved us. (4:19)
- we know that whoever has been born of God does not sin. (5:18)

BASIC BOOK OUTLINE (MAIN DIVISIONS AND SUBDIVISION)
Jesus- seen heard & touched 1:1-4
God is light 1:5-7
Sin can be forgiven 1:8-2:2
walking in the light 2:3-11
3 stages of spiritual growth 2:12-14
Do not love the world 2:15-17
Warning against deception 2:18-27
children of God 2:28-3:3
Sin and the seed 3:4-9
Love one another 3:10-23
Test the spirits 3:24-4:6
Love one another, again 4:7-21
Believing in Jesus 5:1-13
Confidence in prayer 5:14-15
Concluding Remarks 5:16-21

CHAPTER _James 1_

DATE _____

MAIN MESSAGE

Count it all JOY when TRIALS come!

MAIN CHARACTERS

written to the 12 tribes scattered abroad - to the Jewish Christian.

KEY VERSES

James 1:2 Consider it pure joy, my brothers, whenever you face trials of many kinds.
James 1:22 Do not merely listen to the word, and so deceive yourselves. Do what it says.
James 1:15 Then after desire has conceived, it gives birth to sin; and sin when it is full
         grown gives birth to death.

KEY VERSE(S)?
joy - chara - delight
wisdom - sophia - insight
temptation - (vs.12) peirasmos
   trials with a beneficial purpose
                         + effect

COMMANDS?
→ Count it pure joy when trials come. (vs.2)
→ Be quick to listen, slow to speak, slow to
   wrath (vs.19)
→ Get rid of moral filth. (vs.21)
→ Receive word with humility (vs.21)
→ Don't only listen to the word, do
   what it says. (vs.23)

PROMISES?
→ The testing of your faith will
   produce perseverance. (vs.3)
→ Double minded people won't
   receive wisdom. (vs.7-8)
→ The crown of life goes to those
   who persevere. (vs.12)

PRINCIPLES
→ Testing produces maturity. (vs.2-4)
→ Evil desire produces sin & sin produces
   death.
   - sin never starts with death, but
     it always ends with death. (vs.15)
→ keep looking into the word and
   you will do what it says. (vs.25)

BASIC BOOK OUTLINE (MAIN DIVISIONS AND SUBDIVISION)
• GREETINGS   vs.1
• TRIALS + TRIUMPHS   vs.2-8
   Trials produce character 2-4
   wisdom given to those who ask in faith 5-8
• ETERNAL PERSPECTIVES   vs.9-11
   poverty + riches are temporal
• TEMPTATION: GOOD + BAD   vs.12-18
   Those who endure receive the crown of life. 12
   Inward temptations come from lust. 13-14
   God gives good gifts 17-18
• TRIAL'S ENEMIES   vs.19-20
   Quick hearing, slow talking + controlled
   anger overcomes trials.
• DOERS + HEARERS   vs.21-25
   Doers will receive the word with meekness. 21
   Doers aren't deceived. 22
   Doers keep looking into the law. 23-25
• TRUE RELIGION vs.26-27
   A controlled tongue 26
   A compassionate heart 27
   A clean life 27

VERSE REFERENCE ___Josh 1:8___   DATE _____

WRITE OUT THE VERSE, USING A SEPARATE LINE FOR EACH DIVISION OF THOUGHT: (CLUE► DIVISIONS OF THOUGHT OFTEN COME AFTER CONNECTIVE WORDS SUCH AS: AND, BECAUSE, FOR, IF, AND, THEREFORE).

Do not let this Book of the Law depart from your mouth; meditate on it day and night;
So that you may be careful to do everything written in it.
Then you will be prosperous + successful.

KEY WORD(S) - THEIR MEANING?

Law - tōrāh - which means instruction, direction
meditate - hāgāh - which means to moan, utter, speak (25 Xs in O.T.)
prosperous - sāleah - which means to succeed (65 Xs in O.T.)
successful - sâkal - which means to be prudent, act wisely (used 75 Xs in O.T.)

COMMANDS?

Do not let the Bible become obsolete from your daily conversation. meditate on the Bible day and night, which would mean constantly.

PROMISES?

I will be prosperous!
I will be successful!

PRINCIPLES (CAUSE AND EFFECT RELATIONSHIPS)?

If I meditate constantly on the Bible I will be prosperous + successful... meaning I will act wisely.
I won't make dumb moves in life.

WHAT DOES THIS VERSE MEAN TO ME?

If I will follow this simple command God will make my way prosperous. It's as simple as that.
There will be trials + setbacks (John 16:33) but I will overcome! This is a principle of life!

BIBLE CHARACTER _Joseph_   **DATE** _____

REFERENCES _Genesis 37-50_

DESCRIBE THEIR CHILDHOOD EXPERIENCES.

Gen
37

Joseph was the son of Jacob - the 1st son of Jacob's favorite wife
Rachel. Joseph had 11 half-brothers - they were shepherds. He also had
sisters. When Joseph was seventeen he had a dream - a God-given dream.
Joseph was favored by his father as a teenager & his brothers resented
him. Joseph's home was not a perfect home - the animosity that his
brothers had toward him almost got him killed, but instead, they
sold him to some merchant traders.

DESCRIBE GOD'S CALL ON THEIR LIFE.

Gen
37

From the dreams Joseph received it is obvious that God had
called Joseph to be a ruler. For some, God gives them a dream,
For others, a strong desire (like me), for others a vision
(like Paul, Acts 9)

DESCRIBE THEIR RESPONSE TO GOD'S CALL ON THEIR LIFE (POSITIVE AND/OR NEGATIVE).

Joseph seemed to respond well to the dreams he had received.
Eventhough he was ridiculed for his dreams(which may have resulted
from how he let his brothers know about his dreams) he
possessed a positive attitude. This was shown in his attitude
toward his father (Gen 37:13), toward Potiphar (Gen 39:1-6)
toward Potiphar's wife (Gen 39:7-13), toward the prison guard
(39:21-23) and toward the butler & the baker (40:1-23) & toward
the Pharoah (41:14-16) & toward his brothers (Gen 42-45).

OUTLINE THEIR LIFE IN STAGES/SIGNIFICANT TURNING POINTS.

Joseph the Dreamer   37: 5-11

Joseph the worker   37:28, 36 39:1-6

* Joseph the prisoner 39:19 ,   41:13

Joseph the ruler   41: 14-57

* Warren Wiersbe
"Be a Real Teen"

WHAT LESSONS CAN YOU DRAW FOR YOUR LIFE FROM THEIR LIFE?

• Joseph's attitude, through all his trials inspires me.
  - God's job: give me tests ... my job: pass the tests
• The phrase, "and the Lord was with him (39:2-3, 21-23)
  tells me that I can be as close to God as I want. It is "we"
  not "He" who determines how close we get to Him.
• Every God given <u>dream</u> turns into <u>hard work</u>, seasons of
      <u>injustice</u> & ends up in <u>rulership</u>. ATTITUDE IS EVERYTHING!

TOPIC "The Will of God"   DATE _____

KEY REFERENCES	OBSERVATIONS / INSIGHTS / OUTLINES
Matt 7:21-23	The ultimate expression of God's will is that we know Him - not that we prophecy, cast out demons & do wonders.
Phil. 2:13/Heb. 13:21	God will give me the desire to do His will. God actually works in me what is well pleasing in His sight!
Luke 22:42	God's will + my will are not always the same.
John 4:34	God's will is like food - I love to eat! - So I guess I can love this will!
John 6:38-40	God's will for my life in terms of purpose can be defined - Jesus knew what He came to do. Can I define what I came to do?
Rom 12:1-2	God's will - that I offer my body as a living sacrifice. God's will - that I not be conformed to this world.
Heb. 2:4	God's will - that He gave me gifts from the Holy Spirit.
1 Thess. 4:3	God's will - that I avoid sexual immorality
1 Thess 5:16	God's will - that I be joyful all the time
1 Thess 5:18	God's will - that I give thanks in every situation.
Eph. 6:7	whatever I do, do it with all my might.
II Peter 3:9	God's will - that nobody should perish.
Eph. 5:18	God's will - that I be filled with the Spirit.
Eph. 5:17/Col. 1:9	I CAN KNOW WHAT THE WILL OF THE LORD IS! It is not some weird mystery that I have to spend my life trying to discover.
1 John 2:17	He who does God's will lives forever!
Rom. 12:9-21	21 actions for a christian are listed.
Matt. 11:30	The will of God is a yoke that is EASY and it is a burden that is light. LIGHT & EASY - not legalistic & burdensome.

WHAT HAVE I LEARNED?

- The will of God seems to emphasize "who I am" more than "where I go". In other words God's more concerned with my "character" than my "calendar". What college I attend is less important than what kind of person I am at that college.
- The will of God is not a mysterious, unobtainable goal - it can be understood.
- God's will brings more joy than mine, & God gives me the desire for it.
- God's will fits - it's the burden without blisters.

HEED...LEARNING TO MEDITATE

MEDITATION - THE KEY TO GOOD SUCCESS

Meditation is gold digging at its best. Nothing seems to bring more joy than finding nuggets of truth within the pages of the Bible. Remember that we said earlier that the Bible has something "on" it. That something is the "breath" of God. When you meditate on the Word of God, the Holy Spirit takes those words and makes them come alive! Truths and principles begin to jump out at you. The light comes on. You begin to realize truths and insights you already thought you understood. The fact is, you probably did know them (at least in your head), but now you are realizing them in your spirit and in your heart.

God has promised "good success" to those who meditate (Joshua 1:8).

As a 16 year-old teenager, I was challenged to meditate on God's Word. I had attended a *Basic Life Principles* seminar in which the following results of meditation were made clear to me. I was hooked.

Meditation will help you build **God-honoring thought structures.** The Bible tells us that God's thoughts are not our thoughts, nor are His ways our ways (Isaiah 58:8-9). By meditating on God's revealed thoughts and ways in the Bible you begin to align your way of thinking and living to His way of thinking and living. Meditation is, in a sense, a positive expression of brain-washing, having your mind cleansed from a fallen world's way of thinking.

Meditation will help you to **rebuild your emotions.** When you think and act right you begin to feel right. Emotions are the result of your thoughts — think right and you will feel right, think wrong and you will feel wrong. In rebuilding your emotions, you can personalize the scripture you have memorized. For instance, in 1 Timothy 4:15 we read, *"Meditate upon these things, give yourself entirely to them that your progress may be evident to all."*

First Timothy 4:15 personalized would read, "I will meditate upon these things; I (your name) will give myself entirely to them so that my (your name) progress may be evident to all (your friends and family etc.).

Meditation will also help you to **redirect your will.** It has been said that when the "imagination" and the "will" are in conflict the "imagination" will always win. If this is true, then Biblical meditation will eventually affect your "will." As you saturate your "mind" and "emotions" with the Word your "will" will follow. Meditation on the Word of God will build *God-honoring thought structures, rebuild your emotions* and *redirect your will.*

A DEFINITION OF BIBLICAL MEDITATION

Biblical meditation is the act of centering your thoughts upon the Word of God and the God of the Word. The concept behind meditation is that of a cow chewing its cud. As a cow digests its food, it actually brings up the food it has eaten, and eats it again. In the same way, meditation means to digest the Word of God and then bring it up in order to chew on it again. The implication behind this word picture is that the Word of God is so full of spiritual nutrients and blessing, that one consumption would never exhaust the riches found even in one mouthful. Jeremiah said, *"Your words were found, and I did eat them. And your word was to me the joy and rejoicing of my heart"* (Jeremiah 15:16 NKJV). God's Word is real "soul food." Meditation helps you to enjoy every bite.

Biblical meditation is not only a mental exercise, but verbal exercise. The word, meditation in Hebrew is "hagah" which means: *to reflect; to moan, to mutter, to make a quiet sound such as sighing; to meditate or contemplate something as one repeats the words.* To repeat verbally what you are meditating upon will help you to keep your mind from wandering. It will also help you to organize your thoughts and give your ears an opportunity to hear God's Word. Faith comes by hearing (Romans 10:17). Meditation requires the attention of your whole person: *spirit, mind, eyes, ears and mouth.* Solomon says in Proverbs 4:20-22, "My son, give attention to my words; incline your *ear* to my sayings. Do not let them depart from your *eyes*; keep them in the midst of your *heart*; for they are life to those who find them and health to all their flesh." He goes on to say in Proverbs 22:17-18 "Incline your *ear* and hear the words of the wise, and apply your *heart* to my knowledge for it is pleasant if you keep them within you; let them all be fixed on your *lips*" (italics added).

Biblical meditation should not be confused with the Eastern forms of mysticism and meditation such as "transcendental meditation." The issue isn't the actual practice of meditation but the target of one's meditation. In Biblical meditation there is a deliberate focus upon God (Psalm 63:6), God's law (Psalm 1:2; 119:15, 23, 97) and God's works (Psalm 77:12; 143:5).

THE PROMISE

If it weren't for the fact that the Bible is God's Word and therefore true, it would be hard to believe that one simple discipline could produce so many rewards. God declares that if we will meditate on the Word we will have "good success." In Joshua 1:8 we read, *"This book of the Law shall not depart from your mouth, but you shall meditate in it day and night, that you may observe to do according to all that is written in it. For then you will make your way prosperous and then you will have good success"* (NKJV). Under the banner of "good success" what specific success might meditation produce in our lives?

1. PRIVATE STRENGTH

"I have hidden your word in my heart that I might not sin against you"
(Psalm 119:11)

Most sin is not the result of an *outer problem* but an *inner problem*. If you want power over sin, focus on your inside state, not your outside surroundings. Hiding God's Word in your heart will turn you into a transformed person from the "inside out" instead of a conformed person from the "outside in" (Romans 12:1-2).

2. GREAT PEACE

"Great peace have they who love your law, and nothing can make them stumble."
(Psalm 119:165)

Great peace is not the result of outward conditions but the inward condition of the heart. There's something to be said for peaceful circumstances but those times never last too long. That's why we need to meditate so that we can find peace in the Word, because peace never lasts in the world. By the way, this isn't just peace. The promise is for **great peace**. Don't settle for a little bit of peace now and then, believe for a bunch.

3. GREEN EDGE

"...whose leaf does not wither" (Psalm 1:3b).

Have you ever met a "brown edge" believer? You know the kind I'm talking about — edgy kinds of folks. Easily hurt, easily offended, easily tripped? Show me a "brown edge believer" and I'll show you a believer who hasn't meditated on God's Word for some time. There is something about getting your mind and heart cleansed by the Word of God that gives you back your edge, your "green edge."

4. PUBLIC SUCCESS

"Meditate on these things; give yourself entirely to them, that your progress may be evident to all" (1 Timothy 4:15 NKJV).

I remember the first sermon I ever preached. I was 16 years old and the youth pastor asked me to preach to the whole youth group: Jr. High, High School and College. I was scared but I was prepared. After the meeting, a young adult came up to me and said he wanted to be just like me. He saw something in me he wanted. What he saw was the result of meditation. When you meditate on God's Word and give yourself entirely to it, your progress will be evident to everybody, even those older than you. You don't have to blow your own horn, meditation will make progress obvious without you having to promote yourself.

HAVE YOU EVER MET A "BROWN EDGE" BELIEVER?

THE PRACTICE

Memorization and meditation are two different disciplines but they are closely linked together. Memorizing Scripture makes it possible for you to meditate anywhere, at anytime, because you have imprinted the Word *on your mind.* Meditating upon the Word will help you hide it *in your heart.* God offers no rewards for memorization, but He offers "good success" for meditation! In order to memorize the Scripture a few tools are necessary:

1. THE BIBLE

Use the translation or paraphrase with which you are most comfortable. Many students enjoy the New International Version (NIV). Others enjoy the New King James Version (NKJV) because of its poetic yet updated style. "The Message," a paraphrased version of the Bible written in a contemporary syle, is also very popular.

2. A BIBLE CONCORDANCE

A Bible concordance will help you to find other Scriptures that are related to the passage or word upon which you are meditating. Cross referencing will help you get the "big picture" concerning what the Bible has to say in other places about the theme or specific word within the verse or section you are committing to memory.

3. A BIBLE DICTIONARY

A Bible dictionary is just like the normal dictionary except that it focuses specifically on Bible words, customs and teachings. As has already been explained, a Bible dictionary contains a thorough listing of all Bible subjects.

4. 3 X 5 CARDS

I have found 3 X 5 cards to be the most effective tool for memorizing and meditating upon the Word of God. They are easy to take with you wherever you go. I have found them especially helpful when I go on one of my "walks and talks" with God. When memorizing a section of Scripture, I often use a number of cards, writing out a few verses on each card. For memorizing single verses I often put two or three short verses with the same theme on each card. The following "6 Pointers" will get you started on putting together some pretty "lethal" 3 X 5 cards.

A. WRITE OUT A VERSE OR PASSAGE ON THE CARD. Use your own handwriting. It is more personal than typed words. By using your own handwriting you are able to write out key words differently than other words throughout the verse. I usually capitalize all the letters in the key words.

B. RECORD THE DATE YOU BEGIN MEMORIZING THE VERSE(S) ON THE TOP LEFT HAND CORNER. This will help you monitor your progress in memorization and meditation from the date you began.

C. RECORD THE SCRIPTURE REFERENCE(S) IN THE TOP RIGHT HAND CORNER. This will allow you to locate your reference at a glance.

D. HIGHLIGHT, UNDERLINE, COMMENT. Make each card your own personal work of art. Who ever said memorization had to be boring!

E. RECORD THE MEANING OF KEY WORDS ON THE BACK OF THE CARD. Each verse has one or more key words that deserve some study in order to find out their root meanings. For word research use the internet, a concordance or Bible dictionary.

An example of how to use *Strong's Concordance* along with *Vine's Expository Dictionary* is offered below:

EXAMPLE: JOHN 3:16

"For God so loved the world that He gave His one and only Son, that whoever believes in Him shall not perish but have eternal life."

One of the key words in John 3:16 is "loved."

STEP 1 - Look up "loved" in *Strong's Concordance* (found on page 638).

STEP 2 - Find out the number that corresponds to the John 3:16 reference (it happens to be 25).

STEP 3 - Go to the Greek Dictionary found at the back of *Strong's Concordance* and find the number 25. You will discover the Greek word to be *agapao* which means *"to love in a social or moral sense."*

STEP 4 - In order to find out more about this word *agapao* you would need to go to your Bible dictionary. A good choice would be *Vine's Expository Dictionary of Old and New Testament Words* which happens to be keyed to *Strong's* reference numbers. Under the word "love" found in this particular dictionary a whole page is devoted to the word and its different meanings in the Bible. The actual pages of *Strong's Concordance* and *Vine's Expository Dictionary* are shown for your convenience.

STRONG'S

Ps	119:48	thy commandments, which I have l.;	157
Isa	43:4	been honourable, and I have l. thee:	157
Isa	48:14	The Lord hath l. him: he will do his	157
Jer	2:25	I have l. strangers, and after them	157
Jer	8:2	host of heaven, whom they have l.,	157
Jer	14:10	Thus have they l. to wander, they	157
Jer	31:3	I have l. thee with an everlasting	157
Eze	16:37	all them that thou hast l., with all	157
Ho	9:1	l. a reward upon every cornfloor.	157
Ho	9:10	were according as they l.	157
Ho	11:1	Israel was a child, then I l. him, and	157
Mal	1:2	I have l. you, saith the Lord.	157
Mal	1:2	Yet ye say, Wherein hast thou l. us?..	157
Mal	1:2	saith the Lord: yet I l. Jacob,	157
Mal	2:11	the holiness of the Lord which he l.,	157
Mr	10:21	Jesus beholding him l. him, and said..	25
Lu	7:47	many, are forgiven; for she l. much:	.25
Joh	3:16	For God so l. the world, that he	25
Joh	3:19	men l. darkness rather than light,...	25
Joh	11:5	Now Jesus l. Martha, and her sister,	25
Joh	11:36	the Jews, Behold how he l. him!	5368
Joh	12:43	they l. the praise of men more than..	25
Joh	13:1	having l. his own which were in the..	25
Joh	13:1	the world, he l. them unto the end.	25
Joh	13:23	one of his disciples, whom Jesus l.	25
Joh	13:34	as I have l. you, that ye also love	25
Joh	14:21	loveth me shall be l. of my Father,	25
Joh	14:28	If ye l. me, ye would rejoice, because	25
Joh	15:9	As the Father hath l. me, so have I	25
Joh	15:9	me, so have I l. you: continue ye in	25
Joh	15:12	ye love one another, as I have l. you	25
Joh	16:27	because ye have l. me, and have	5368
Joh	17:23	and hast l. them, as thou hast l. me.	25
Joh	17:26	the love wherewith thou hast l. me	25
Joh	19:26	the disciple standing by whom he l.,	25

GREEK

24. ἀγανάκτησις **aganaktēsis**, *ag-an-ak'-tay-sis*; from 23; *indignation:*—indignation.

25. ἀγαπάω **agapaō**, *ag-ap-ah'-o*; perh. from ἄγαν **agan** (*much*) [or comp. 5689]; to *love* (in a social or moral sense):—(be-) love (-ed). Comp. 5368.

26. ἀγάπη **agapē**, *ag-ah'-pay*; from 25; *love*, i.e. *affection* or *benevolence*; spec. (plur.) a *love-feast:*—(feast of) charity ([-ably]), dear, love.

VINES

LOVE (Noun and Verb)
A. Verbs.

1. *agapaō* (ἀγαπάω, 25) and the corresponding noun *agapē* (B, No. 1 below) present "the characteristic word of Christianity, and since the Spirit of revelation has used it to express ideas previously unknown, inquiry into its use, whether in Greek literature or in the Septuagint, throws but little light upon its distinctive meaning in the NT. Cf., however, Lev. 19:18; Deut. 6:5.

"*Agapē* and *agapaō* are used in the NT (*a*) to describe the attitude of God toward His Son, John 17:26; the human race, generally, John 3:16; Rom 5:8; and to such as believe on the Lord Jesus Christ, particularly, John 14:21; (*b*) to convey His will to His children concerning their attitude one toward another, John 13:34, and toward all men, 1 Thess. 3:12; 1 Cor. 16:14; 2 Pet. 1:7; (*c*) to express the essential nature of God, 1 John 4:8.

"Love can be known only from the actions it prompts. God's love is seen in the gift of His Son, 1 John 4:9, 10. But obviously this is not the love of complacency, or affection, that is, it was not drawn out by any excellency in its objects, Rom. 5:8. It was an exercise of the divine will in deliberate choice, made without assignable cause save that which lies in the nature of God Himself, Cf. Deut. 7:7, 8.

"Love had its perfect expression among men in the Lord Jesus Christ, 2 Cor. 5:14; Eph. 2:4; 3:19; 5:2; Christian love is the fruit of His Spirit in the Christian, Gal. 5:22.

"Christian love has God for its primary object, and expresses itself first of all in implicit obedience to His commandments, John 14:15, 21, 23; 15:10; 1 John 2:5; 5:3; 2 John 6. Self-will, that is, self-pleasing, is the negation of love to God.

"Christian love, whether exercised toward the brethren, or toward men generally, is not an impulse from the feelings, it does not always run with the natural inclinations, nor does it spend itself only upon those for whom some affinity is discovered. Love seeks the welfare of all, Rom. 15:2, and works no ill to any, 13:8–10; love seeks opportunity to do good to 'all men, and especially toward them that are of the household of the faith,' Gal. 6:10. See further 1 Cor. 13 and Col. 3:12–14."*

In respect of *agapaō* as used of God, it expresses the deep and constant "love" and interest of a perfect Being towards entirely unworthy objects, producing and fostering a reverential "love" in them towards the Giver, and a practical "love" towards those who are partakers of the same, and a desire to help others to seek the Giver. See BELOVED.

METHODS OF MEMORIZATION

Memorization is a scary word to many. What some refer to as a "mental block" is often nothing more than an "ambition block." We memorize the things that we want to memorize! Important phone numbers and names are not easily forgotten. I've challenged many young people throughout the nation, to memorize Psalms 1 within one day, during a weekend conference or camp. Many have met the challenge and received the reward-a free t-shirt, hat, or **BBC** Manual, etc. The rewards of Bible meditation are far greater than a baseball hat or t-shirt. We will meet the *requirements* when we understand the *rewards*. The methods below will help you to memorize.

REPEAT THE VERSE. Repetition is the most tried and proven method of memorization. Repeat the verse out loud three to five times. Divide the verse into some form of rhythm, emphasizing key words or key phrases. Make use of "space learning" which is nothing more than repeating the verse throughout a section of time (throughout the hour, the morning, the afternoon, the evening or the whole day) leaving space between repetitions. I have found that I learn a verse the quickest when I attack it in phrases, over-emphasizing certain phrases based on the sentence structure.

FORM ACRONYMS. Take the initial letters of key words in a verse to form an acrostic. When I memorized Philippians 4:8 "Finally brethren, whatever things are true, whatever things are noble, whatever things are just, whatever things are pure, whatever things are lovely, whatever things are of good report, if there is any virtue, if there is anything praiseworthy — meditate on these things" (NKJV). I took the key words: true, noble, just, lovely, good report, virtue, praiseworthy and created the acrostic, TNJL-GRVP. I then created a rhythm by bunching the letters in two groups of three and one group of two: TNJ, LGR, VP. The last two letters represented in my mind, Vice President. This list was quickly and easily memorized.

DEVELOP ASSOCIATIONS. For many, this method of memorization works well. The strategy involves linking an unknown to a known. When learning a new verse or section of Scripture you associate a familiar mental picture with a certain part of the verse or verses. For instance, if you were to memorize 1 Corinthians 13:4-8, you might picture a turtle for verse 4 (love is patient), a filing cabinet for verse 5 (keeps no record of wrong), a fireworks display for verse 6 (rejoices in the truth), a policeman for verse 7 (love always protects), and a sunrise for verse 8 (love never fails).

SCRIPTURE IN SONG. Putting scripture to a familiar tune or a made-up melody can be very effective. Do you remember learning your ABC's to a tune when you started school? Scripture put to music can now be purchased online or at your local Christian bookstore. If you can't find what you are looking for, come up with your own tunes for the Scriptures you want to memorize. If you enjoy this method why not go for it — *sing* your way into memorization and meditation.

THE PLAN

Throughout your lifetime you will go through phases. At times you will approach your devotions and the memorization of Scripture with gusto. Then there will be those dry seasons where you will almost question your salvation. Take heart, you aren't alone. Everyone goes through ups and downs for all kinds of reasons. One of those reasons is a change in schedule. I will never forget the turmoil I faced when I graduated from Jr. High to the big world of High School. Because my high school was a long way away, my daily schedule and rhythm changed dramatically. I wasn't able to have my devotions at the same time each day as I did as a Jr. High student. It almost devastated me until I realized that God didn't care when I had my quiet time as much as He was concerned that I had one. With some adjusting, I was able to get back on track again. Changes in lifestyle, age, environment and maturity affect the different phases of our lives. Learn to flow with the changes without losing sight of your priority. Remember, the goal of your memorization and meditation is to know God and be more like Jesus — *"I shall be satisfied when I awake with your likeness"* (Psalm 17:15b) — not to win brownie points.

GOALS, GOALS, GOALS

Goals are intimidating creatures because by nature they are measurable. A good goal can be measured by "time" and "performance." To help you understand the difference between good goals and bad goals consider the following statement. "I want to memorize Scripture." Is this a good goal or a bad goal? The answer — a bad goal! Why? Because it cannot be measured. Now study this statement. "I want to memorize one verse per week for the next year." Is this a good goal or a bad goal? The answer - a good goal! Why? Because it's measurable by time (one year) and performance (one verse per week). Goal setting is often nerve racking because it sets us up for the possibility of failure. For this reason it is wise to set goals that are attainable.

When setting goals it is important to be able to see the *goal line*. In other words, it is important to begin with the "end in mind." As you picture on the screen of your mind the end result, you have created an image worth shooting for. In the **FEED** section you were given the **DEVOTIONAL CHALLENGE**. In this section why not go for the **MEMORIZATION AND MEDITATION CHART**. The difference between success and failure for many is often nothing more than a simple chart. By using the chart, you will be able to **see** your progress. Remember if you don't reach your goal the first time, try again. Success is failing ten times and getting up eleven. Go for it — commit yourself to at least one verse a week for the next year. You will not be disappointed.

THE MEDITATION CHALLENGE

CHALLENGE #1

Memorize and meditate upon one verse (or short section) per week for the next year plus, memorize and meditate upon one key chapter or section of scripture (every month) for the next year.

CHALLENGE #2

Memorize and meditate upon one verse (or short section) per week for the next year.

ONE YEAR MEMORIZATION/MEDITATION CHART

CHALLENGE #1

Memorize and meditate upon one verse (or short section) per week for the next year plus, memorize and meditate upon one key chapter or section of scripture (every month) for the next year.

CHALLENGE #2

Memorize and meditate upon one verse (or short section) per week for the next year.

NOTE: While reading the Bible you may come across certain verses that you would rather commit to memory than the ones suggested. Write those references on the dotted line provided in each box.

❑ 1 JOSH 1:8	❑ 2 1 COR 15:58	❑ 3 ISA 53:6	❑ 4 PHIL 2:3-4
❑ 5 2 CHRON. 7:14	❑ 6 JER 29:11	❑ 7 JOHN 15:16	❑ 8 PROV 3:5-6
❑ 9 ACTS 1:8	❑ 10 ROM 6:23	❑ 11 ISA 55:6-7	❑ 12 JOEL 2:28
❑ 13 2 COR. 5:17	❑ 14 EPH 6:10-11	❑ 15 1 JOHN 1:9	❑ 16 MAL 3:10
❑ 17 JOHN 10:10	❑ 18 EPH 6:12	❑ 19 1 JOHN 3:9	❑ 20 MARK 16:15
❑ 21 ROM 10:12-13	❑ 22 EPH 6:13	❑ 23 HEB 13:8	❑ 24 GAL 2:20
❑ 25 1 PET 2:9	❑ 26 PSA 32:1-2	❑ 27 JAMES 1:5	❑ 28 1 TIM 4:12
❑ 29 JOHN 3:16	❑ 30 MATT 6:33	❑ 31 1 THES 4:3-4	❑ 32 1 COR 10:13
❑ 33 1 JOHN 3:16	❑ 34 PSA 27:1	❑ 35 ROM 12:1-2	❑ 36 JER 29:13
❑ 37 ECC 12:1	❑ 38 HEB 11:6	❑ 39 ISA 40:31	❑ 40 PHIL 4:6-7
❑ 41 JER 15:16	❑ 42 1 COR. 13:4-5	❑ 43 PSA 18:2	❑ 44 PHIL 4:8
❑ 45 ISA 41:10	❑ 46 1 COR 13:6-7	❑ 47 ROM 3:23	❑ 48 PSA 37:4-5
❑ 49 PSA 84:11	❑ 50 HEB 4:12	❑ 51 1 JOHN 4:7-8	❑ 52 REV 3:20

TURNING YOUR BEDROOM INTO A BIBLE COLLEGE

Thirty-five key chapters or sections of Scripture listed below are suggested for memorization and meditation. Of the 35, 13 have been recorded on the following pages including a sample page of my notes and insights gained from Psalm 1. Document your insights right on the page using the principles of observation laid out earlier in this manual. "Mark up" this manual and it will become a treasured piece for years to come, bearing your own personal touch. Remember, sometimes the only difference between success and failure is a simple tool. Could it be that the **BBC** Manual will be that simple tool that got you hooked on a discipline that will change the course of your life? Let it launch you into a discipline of devotion, memorization and meditation.

SUGGESTED KEY SECTIONS/ CHAPTERS OF SCRIPTURE

Psalm 1 - Meditation/Rewards

Psalm 23 - The Great Shepherd

Psalm 139:1-18 - God's Thoughts about You

Joshua 1:1-9 - God's Commission to Joshua

Isaiah 53:1-7 - Jesus the Suffering Lamb

Isaiah 55:6-11 - God's Mercy to Man

Amos 8:11-12 - God's Word is Food

Malachi 3:16-18 - Fearing the Lord

Matthew 5:1-10, 11-16 - The Beatitudes

John 15:1-18 - The True Vine

John 17 - The Lord's Prayer

Acts 2:42-47 - The Church Grows

Romans 6:11-14 - Dead to Sin

Romans 8 - Freedom from Condemnation

Romans 12:1-8 - Living Sacrifices

1 Corinthians 13:4-8 - Real Love

Galatians 5:16-26 - Walking in the Spirit

Ephesians 1:15-23 - Spiritual Wisdom

Ephesians 2:1-11 - God's Grace

Ephesians 6:10-18 - The Armor of God

Philippians 2:3-11 - The Mind of Christ

Philippians 3:7-16 - Pressing On

Philippians 4:6-20 - Meditate on these Things

Colossians 3 - Focusing Your Emotions

1 Thessalonians 4:1-7 - Purity

1 Timothy 3:1-13

   - Qualifications for Spiritual Leaders

1 Timothy 4:12-16 - A Word to the Young

2 Timothy 2:1-7 - Be Strong in Grace

Hebrews 12:1-2 - The Faith Race

James 1 - Marks of Maturity

1 Peter 4:12-19 - Suffering for God

1 Peter 5:5-11

   - Submit to God/Resist the Devil

2 Peter 1:5-11 - Add to Your Faith…

1 John 2:15-17 - Love not the World

Blessed is the man

who does not walk in the counsel of

the wicked

or stand in the way of sinners

or sit in the seat of mockers.

²But his delight is in the law of the Lord,

and on his law he meditates day

and night.

³He is like a tree planted by streams of

water,

which yields its fruit in season

and whose leaf does not wither.

Whatever he does prospers.

⁴Not so the wicked!

They are like chaff

that the wind blows away.

⁵Therefore the wicked will not stand in

the judgment,

nor sinners in the assembly of the

righteous.

⁶For the Lord watches over the way of

the righteous,

but the way of the wicked will

perish.

Handwritten annotations:

Blessed: happy, envious, fortunate ze. Happy people have Godly friends.

covers all activity in life

ya'as - advice to plan, purpose to counsel, to advise

what are delights to me? SKIING ICE CREAM SUNDAE. The Bible can mean more to me than these YES!

a contrast

meditation more than memorization (hah-gah) #1897 to reflect, to moan

more than written law, but the lifestyle of God's people.

expressing vitality and life, none of this brown edge believer stuff

you can be a tree or chaff, one is planted, the other blows away. (contrast!)

we're talking the real thing here.

contrast

cause and effect

the Lord is watching over us, not to find something wrong but to guide & protect

let all your enemies perish oh Lord

Hebrew abad (ah-vahd) strongs #6 - be ruined... be destroyed sounds pretty final doesn't it?

KEY WORD(S)

- Blessed - aŝrê means blessed, happy, state of prosperity or happiness that comes when a superior bestows his blessing on one.
- Delight - hēpes means pleasure, desire
- meditates - hāgāh means to murmer, growl, speak. The Jewish people in the time of David meditated by repeating phrases over and over.
- Prospers - sālēah means to succeed. The source is God (2 chron. 26:5)
- way - derek means path, road, highway, a manner of behavior

CROSS REFERENCES

Prov. 4:14, Jer. 15:17, Psa. 119:14, Josh. 1:8, Zach 6:13

Gen 39:2,3,23, Psa. 37:8, Nahum 1:7, II Tim 2:19

Judges 5:31

COMMANDS?

PROMISES?

meditators on God's law will be planted by streams of water.

meditators on God's law will be fruitful in their season.

meditators on God's law will not have withering leaves (no brown edges).

meditators on God's law will prosper in whatever they do.

PRINCIPLES?

meditation produces stability of life. (vs. 3)

MY PRAYER

Dear Lord... help me to always find my delight in your word and in your ways. Cause me to always seek counsel from the right source. Thank you for giving me the desire to delight in your word.

PSALM 23

[1]·The Lord is my shepherd, I shall lack nothing.

[2]·He makes me lie down in green pastures,

he leads me beside quiet waters,

[3]·he restores my soul.

He guides me in paths of righteousness

for his name's sake.

[4]·Even though I walk

through the valley of the shadow of death,

I will fear no evil,

for you are with me;

your rod and your staff,

they comfort me.

[5]·You prepare a table before me

in the presence of my enemies.

You anoint my head with oil;

my cup overflows.

[6]·Surely goodness and love will follow me

all the days of my life,

and I will dwell in the house of the

Lord forever.

KEY WORD(S)

CROSS REFERENCES

COMMANDS?

PROMISES?

PRINCIPLES?

MY PRAYER

ISAIAH 53:1-7

1 Who has believed our message

and to whom has the arm of the Lord been revealed?

2 He grew up before him like a tender shoot,

and like a root out of dry ground.

He had no beauty or majesty to attract us to him,

nothing in his appearance that we

should desire him.

3 He was despised and rejected by men,

a man of sorrows, and familiar with suffering.

Like one from whom men hide their faces

he was despised, and we esteemed him not.

4 Surely he took up our infirmities

and carried our sorrows,

yet we considered him stricken by God,

smitten by him and afflicted.

5 But he was pierced for our transgressions,

he was crushed for our iniquities;

the punishment that brought us peace was upon him,

and by his wounds we are healed.

6 We all, like sheep, have gone astray,

each of us had turned to his own way;

and the Lord has laid on him

the iniquity of us all.

7 He was oppressed and afflicted,

yet he did not open his mouth;

he was led like a lamb to the slaughter,

and as a sheep before her shearers is silent,

so he did not open his mouth.

KEY WORD(S)

CROSS REFERENCES

COMMANDS?

PROMISES?

PRINCIPLES?

MY PRAYER

MATTHEW 5:1-10

[1] Now when he saw the crowds, he
went up on a mountainside and sat
down. His disciples came to him, [2] and he
began to teach them, saying:
[3] "Blessed are the poor in spirit,
for theirs is the kingdom of heaven.
[4] Blessed are those who mourn,
for they will be comforted.
[5] Blessed are the meek,
for they will inherit the earth.
[6] Blessed are those who hunger and
thirst for righteousness,
for they will be filled.
[7] Blessed are the merciful,
for they will be shown mercy.
[8] Blessed are the pure in heart,
for they will see God.
[9] Blessed are the peacemakers,
for they will be called sons of God.
[10] Blessed are those who are persecuted
because of righteousness,
for theirs is the kingdom of heaven."

KEY WORD(S)

CROSS REFERENCES

COMMANDS?

PROMISES?

PRINCIPLES?

MY PRAYER

THE BBC MANUAL

MATTHEW 5:11-16

11 "Blessed are you when people insult you, persecute you and falsely say all kinds of evil against you because of me. 12 Rejoice and be glad, because great is your reward in heaven, for in the same way they persecuted the prophets who were before you.

13 You are the salt of the earth. But if the salt loses its saltiness, how can it be made salty again? It is no longer good for anything, except to be thrown out and trampled by men.

14 You are the light of the world. A city on a hill cannot be hidden. 15 Neither do people light a lamp and put it under a bowl. Instead they put it on its stand, and it gives light to everyone in the house. 16 In the same way, let your light shine before men, that they may see your good deeds and praise your Father in heaven.

KEY WORD(S)

CROSS REFERENCES

COMMANDS?

PROMISES?

PRINCIPLES?

MY PRAYER

1 CORINTHIANS 13:4-8

4 Love is patient, love is kind. It does not
envy, it does not boast, it is not proud. 5 It
is not rude, it is not self-seeking, it is not
easily angered, it keeps no record of
wrongs. 6 Love does not delight in evil but
rejoices with the truth. 7 It always protects,
always trusts, always hopes, always perseveres.
8 Love never fails. But where there are
prophecies, they will cease; where there
are tongues, they will be stilled; where
there is knowledge; it will pass away.

TURNING YOUR
BEDROOM
INTO A BIBLE
COLLEGE

KEY WORD(S)

CROSS REFERENCES

COMMANDS?

PROMISES?

PRINCIPLES?

MY PRAYER

GALATIANS 5:16-26

16 So, I say, live by the Spirit, and you
will not gratify the desires of the sinful
nature. 17 For the sinful nature desires
what is contrary to the Spirit, and the
Spirit what is contrary to the sinful nature.
They are in conflict with each other,
so that you do not do what you want. 18 But
if you are led by the Spirit, you are not
under law.
19 The acts of the sinful nature are obvious:
Sexual immorality, impurity and debauchery;
20 idolatry and witchcraft; hatred, discord, jealousy,
fits of rage, self ambition, dissensions, factions 21 and
envy; drunkenness, orgies, and the like. I warn you,
as I did before, that those who live like this will
not inherit the kingdom of God.
22 But the fruit of the Spirit is love, joy, peace,
patience, kindness, goodness, faithfulness,
23 gentleness and self-control. Against such
things there is no law.
24 Those who belong to Christ Jesus have
crucified the sinful nature with its
passions and desires. 25 Since we live by the
Spirit, let us keep in step with the Spirit.
26 Let us not become conceited, provoking
and envying each other.

KEY WORD(S)

CROSS REFERENCES

COMMANDS?

PROMISES?

PRINCIPLES?

MY PRAYER

EPHESIANS 6:10-18

10 Finally, be strong in the Lord and in his mighty power. 11 Put on the full armor of God so that you can take your stand against the devil's schemes. 12 For our struggle is not against flesh and blood, but against the rulers, against the authorities, against the powers of this dark world and against the spiritual forces of evil in the heavenly realms. 13 Therefore put on the full armor of God, so that when the day of evil comes, you may be able to stand your ground, and after you have done everything, to stand. 14 Stand firm then, with the belt of truth buckled around your waist, with the breastplate of righteousness in place, 15 and with your feet fitted with the readiness that comes from the gospel of peace. 16 In addition to all this, take up the shield of faith, with which you can extinguish all the flaming arrows of the evil one. 17 Take the helmet of salvation and the sword of the Spirit, which is the word of God. 18 And pray in the Spirit on all occasions with all kinds of prayers and requests. With this in mind, be alert and always keep on praying for all the saints.

KEY WORD(S)

CROSS REFERENCES

COMMANDS?

PROMISES?

PRINCIPLES?

MY PRAYER

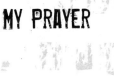

PHILIPPIANS 2:3-11

3 Do nothing out of selfish ambition or vain conceit,
but in humility consider others better
than yourselves. 4 Each of you should look
not only to your own interests, but also to
the interests of others.
5 Your attitude should be the same as
that of Christ Jesus:
6 Who, being in very nature God,
did not consider equality with God
something to be grasped,
7 but made himself nothing,
taking the very nature of a servant,
being made in human likeness.
8 And being found in appearance as a man,
he humbled himself
and became obedient to death—
even death on a cross!
9 Therefore God exalted him to the highest place
and gave him the name that is
above every name,
10 that at the name of Jesus every knee
should bow,
in heaven and on earth and under the earth,
11 and every tongue confess that Jesus Christ is Lord,
to the glory of God the Father.

KEY WORD(S)

CROSS REFERENCES

COMMANDS?

PROMISES?

PRINCIPLES?

MY PRAYER

2 PETER 1:5-11

5 For this very reason, make every effort
to add to your faith goodness; and to
goodness, knowledge; 6 and to knowledge,
self-control; and to self-control, perseverance;
and to perseverance, godliness; 7 and to godliness,
brotherly kindness; and to brotherly kindness, love.
8 For if you possess these qualities in increasing measure,
they will keep you from being ineffective
and unproductive in your knowledge of
our Lord Jesus Christ. 9 But if anyone does not have
them, he is nearsighted and blind, and has forgotten
that he has been cleansed from his past sins.
10 Therefore, my brothers, be all the more
eager to make your calling and
election sure. For if you do these things,
you will never fall, 11 and you will receive
a rich welcome into the eternal kingdom
of our Lord and Savior Jesus Christ.

KEY WORD(S)

CROSS REFERENCES

COMMANDS?

PROMISES?

PRINCIPLES?

MY PRAYER

1 JOHN 2:15-17

15 Do not love the world or anything in the world. If anyone loves the world, the love of the Father is not in him. 16 For everything in the world— the cravings of sinful man, the lust of his eyes and the boasting of what he has and does—comes not from the Father but from the world. 17 The world and its desires pass away, but the man who does the will of God lives forever.

KEY WORD(S)

CROSS REFERENCES

COMMANDS?

PROMISES?

PRINCIPLES?

MY PRAYER

COLOSSIANS 3:12-17

12 Therefore, as God's chosen people, holy and dearly loved, clothe yourselves with compassion, kindness, humility, gentleness and patience. 13 Bear with each other and forgive whatever grievances you may have against one another. Forgive as the Lord forgave you. 14 And over all these virtues put on love, which binds them all together in perfect unity.

15 Let the peace of Christ rule in your hearts, since as members of one body you were called to peace. And be thankful. 16 Let the word of Christ dwell in you richly as you teach and admonish one another with all wisdom, and as you sing psalms, hymns and spiritual songs with gratitude in your hearts to God. 17 And whatever you do, whether in word or deed, do it all in the name of the Lord Jesus, giving thanks to God the Father through him.

TURNING YOUR BEDROOM INTO A BIBLE COLLEGE

KEY WORD(S)

CROSS REFERENCES

COMMANDS?

PROMISES?

PRINCIPLES?

MY PRAYER

PHILIPPIANS 3:7-16

7 But whatever was to my profit I now consider loss for the sake of Christ. 8 What is more, I consider everything a loss compared to the surpassing greatness of knowing Christ Jesus my Lord, for whose sake I have lost all things. I consider them rubbish, that I may gain Christ 9 and be found in him, not having a righteousness of my own that comes from the law, but that which is through faith in Christ—the righteousness that comes from God and is by faith. 10 I want to know Christ and the power of his resurrection and the fellowship of sharing in his sufferings, becoming like him in his death, 11 and so, somehow, to attain to the resurrection from the dead.

12 Not that I have already obtained all this, or have already been made perfect, but I press on to take hold of that for which Christ Jesus took hold of me. 13 Brothers, I do not consider myself yet to have taken hold of it. But one thing I do: Forgetting what is behind and straining toward what is ahead, 14 I press on toward the goal to win the prize for which God has called me heavenward in Christ Jesus.

TURNING YOUR BEDROOM INTO A BIBLE COLLEGE

KEY WORD(S)

CROSS REFERENCES

COMMANDS?

PROMISES?

PRINCIPLES?

MY PRAYER

THE DOUBLE CHALLENGE

15 MINUTES OF DEVOTIONAL BIBLE READING **+15** MINUTES OF MEMORIZATION AND MEDITATION **=30** MINUTES A DAY IN GOD'S WORD!

"One half hour a day. I don't think I could ever find the time to do it! Where will I find the time to make it happen?" This could very well be your initial reaction to such a challenge — but guess what — God is a debtor to no man. What you give to God in time, He will make up in more time given back to you. I'll never forget that Wednesday evening at church. I was about 16 at the time and John (one of the youth group members a few years older than me) was sharing a testimony about how he was thinking about not showing up for the Bible study that night. He said that the Lord told him that if he would go to Bible study that He (the Lord) would give him back more time than he spent by attending the Bible study. For some reason, it meant a lot to me that night. I still remember that moment many years later. I think the Lord wanted me to realize at an early age, that whatever I give to Him, He will return in greater amounts than I have given. In relationship to this challenge, you may not understand it, but you won't even miss the time. As a matter of fact, you'll end up getting more accomplished, with time to spare. One half hour given to God in devotion and meditation will produce His blessing on the remaining 23 1/2 hours. This beats 24 hours of time without His blessing. The Lord multiplies back to us whatever we give to Him. Luke 6:38 tells us,

"Give and it will be given to you. A good measure, pressed down, shaken together and running over will be poured into your lap."

GO FOR IT!
CHOOSE THE CHALLENGE!

DEED... LEARNING TO APPLY

It is quite possible to become a scholar of the Bible and never be changed by it. So far you have gained skill in learning how to **observe** and **meditate**. Now you must submit yourself to **apply** or put into practice the things you have learned.

Application is the most challenging yet the most natural part of a devotional walk with God. Challenging because we are people who miss the mark easily, for all of us have sinned and come short of God's best. Natural because the "root" determines the "fruit." Jesus said in John 15:5a, *"I am the vine; you are the branches. If a man remains in me and I in him, he will bear much fruit…"* Fruit is a natural by-product of the root. Have you ever seen an apple tree "sweat" apples? No. The root determines the fruit. In the same way that a tree naturally produces fruit, so will our lives if we stay connected.

I can still remember it vividly in my mind. I told God that I wanted Him to get my dad a new job in a different city so I could start all over again. I had just become a teenager, we were fairly new to the neighborhood but I already had a bad reputation for being a big mouth. I thought the answer might be

relocation. It wasn't. I decided to take matters into my own hands and made a decision to change my reputation all on my own. My battle plan was to literally, physically shut my mouth at school, and literally, physically never open it. You can't be called a loud mouth if your mouth is shut, can you? I made it to the noon hour and my friend Ken said, "You haven't spoken all day." My response was silence. I'm pretty sure that the Lord was somewhat amused by me "sweating it." He came to my rescue though and offered me a better approach — meditation, devotion, time spent in His presence and abiding. Within months, things began to change from the inside out, not because of "lock jaw."

Things change when **we** change. Much of *application* is the result of *transformation*. Yet the first step to *transformation* is *information*. That's why we need to learn the skills of *observation* and *meditation*. I'm happy to say that the Lord cleaned up my mouth. Oh, I still use it, but better things come out of it now. Getting God's Word into my heart is what made the difference!

LEARNING TO APPLY

In 2 Timothy 3:16-17, Paul tells us what the Bible does for us. *"All Scripture is God-breathed and is useful for teaching, rebuking, correcting and training in righteousness, so that the man of God may be thoroughly equipped for every good work."* This verse states the reason for the Bible. It was written to equip us for application. Words like *teaching, rebuking, correcting* and *training* often bring up negative emotions based on previous unpleasant experiences. We have all been beaten up by guilt and condemnation, some of it false, some of it true. The encouraging note in this is the first five words, "All Scripture is God breathed." This means that every *teaching, rebuking, correcting* and *training* moment in the Bible has life in it. It has God's breath. His breath *breathes* life. When God breathed into Adam, he became a living soul (Genesis 2:7). The Word of God is alive and calls for a response of the heart. God's Word either softens hearts or hardens hearts; depending upon the attitude of the heart. *"Today if you will hear His voice, do not harden your hearts"* (Hebrews 3:7-8).

THE APPLY PLAN

In developing an apply plan you need to ask some questions and find some answers. The following three questions cover the bases.

- What am I to believe?
- What am I to be?
- What am I to do?

WHAT AM I TO BELIEVE? What you believe is of utmost importance. Out of your *true beliefs* come your *traceable actions*. When you read, study or meditate on the Word of God ask yourself what am I to believe about God, Jesus Christ, the Holy Spirit, faith, forgiveness, salvation, sin, etc.? There are two kinds of believing. One is mere intellectual assent and the other is deep-settled absolute conviction. Go for the second one. It takes more effort to develop but it brings much more fruit. Many of the things we believe are somewhere between intellectual assent and heartfelt conviction. Meditation is what moves what we believe 18 inches south from our heads to our hearts.

WHAT AM I TO BE? This question focuses upon our "attitude." A positive attitude is the result of meditation. People who meditate on God's Word have better attitudes than people who don't. "Being" brings us back to the fruit tree illustration. Pear trees produce pears because they are pear trees. They don't "do" pears, they "bear" pears because they are pear trees. In the same way we don't "do" fruit we "bear" fruit. Isn't it interesting that the Bible speaks of the "works" or "deeds" of the flesh but never about the "works" or "deeds" of the Spirit. Rather, the Bible speaks of the "fruit" of the Spirit, "works" are produced by the flesh. By the way, have you noticed, we're not called "human doings" we're called "human beings." Now there's something to meditate upon.

WHAT AM I TO DO? This question focuses on our "actions." When we hear the word "actions" we usually think about things such as projects, accomplishments, facts, figures, deadlines, etc. These are all fine and dandy things to think about, but much of the "action" in the Bible focuses upon relationships. The Bible is a book about God's relationship with man, and man's relationship with others. While the Bible emphasizes *relationship*, the church often emphasizes *belief*. Throughout history, battles have been carried out under the banner of "this" belief or "that" interpretation. Concern for "right beliefs" has divided marriages, families, churches and even denominations. The emphasis of the Bible is "right relationships." A right relationship with God through Jesus Christ and a right relationship with my fellow man, my world and myself. Isn't it comforting to know that God puts such an emphasis upon healthy relationships? It makes you want to know Him, love Him and serve Him.

PSALM 15

"Lord who may dwell in your sanctuary? Who may live on your holy hill? He whose walk is blameless and who does what is righteous, who speaks the truth from his heart and has no slander on his tongue, who does his neighbor no wrong and casts no slur on his fellow man, who despises a vile man but honors those who fear the Lord, who keeps his oath even when it hurts. Who lends his money without usury and does not accept a bribe against the innocent. He who does these things will never be shaken."

Where is the emphasis placed when it comes to who can live where God lives? The answer — relationship. If you want to live in God's neighborhood you have to love people.

I can remember as a teenager, reading a book called, *"Strategy for Living"* by Ed Dayton and Ted Engstrom. In that book I learned the difference between a purpose and a goal. A purpose is an aim or direction, something we want to achieve, those immeasurable ideals and ultimate desires of our heart. For instance the purpose of my life is to **"KNOW GOD AND MAKE HIM KNOWN."** This is a wonderful purpose but a lousy goal. Do you remember the difference between good goals and bad goals? Good goals can be measured and bad goals cannot be measured.

Let's develop a scenario to help us walk through the process of applying the Word to our lives.

STEP 1 - DETERMINE YOUR PURPOSE/OBJECTIVE

After having read through this manual you may have decided you want a healthy devotional life. Your objective could be defined as follows: **"I WANT A HEALTHY DEVOTIONAL LIFE."** Objectives are easier to define because they are general, immeasurable ideals. Step 2 is where the greater work begins.

STEP 2 - DEFINE YOUR GOALS

Defining goals is a challenging business because we are actually setting ourselves up for the possibility of failure. The greatest fear shouldn't be in trying and failing, but in failing to try! Don't be afraid of falling short, fear not getting up to try again. The other challenging aspect of goal setting is that it requires measurable action.

STEP 3 - DEVELOP YOUR ACTION PLAN

Developing an action plan involves defining the nitty gritty details that seem very elementary yet are essential in the process of accomplishing your overall objectives or purpose. Under each goal you can determine which kinds of actions you will need to do in order to reach your goals. Check out the staircase for a clearer picture of the process.

The following diagram will help you to see the progression towards fulfilling your objectives. Think of the fulfillment of your objective as climbing a staircase. The only way to the top is to take the steps.

THE STAIRCASE
OVERALL OBJECTIVE: I WANT A HEALTHY DEVOTIONAL LIFE

3

GOAL #3

I will memorize and meditate upon at least one verse per week for one year.

ACTION POINTS

- I will purchase 3 x 5 cards and fluorescent marker pens.
- I will rehearse my verse(s) with a friend once per week.

2

GOAL #2

I will turn my bedroom into a Bible College.

ACTION POINTS

- I will put a **WORD ON THE WALL** poster on my bedroom wall.
- I will purchase a small desk.

1

GOAL #1

I will spend 15 minutes per day reading my Bible for one year.

ACTION POINTS

- I will purchase a Study Bible and three study tools.
- I will determine what time of day I will spend with the Lord.
- I won't receive any cell phone calls during my quiet time.

As you can tell, reaching your objective is a process. One step at a time will get you to your desired destination. Putting a date on each of your action points is a key to seeing your goals realized. Many lofty intentions and New Year's resolutions never got off the ground because someone didn't define their goals and develop their action plans to get them to the top!

ACCOUNTABILITY

No man is an island and following Jesus is not just a "personal thing." The Bible calls us into relationship with one another. Can you imagine one of your knees giving out in a marathon, and when asked by the other knee what had happened, the knee responded, "Oh, it's just a personal thing." We all know knees don't talk but the point is obvious: Christians are called the Body of Christ and each part of the body has an essential role to play in relation to the other parts. We all need each other for encouragement, support and correction. I can remember as a young boy my dad and I would throw the football in the backyard. I'll have to admit when my dad was throwing me the ball, I tried harder. We naturally try harder when we are being watched by those we love and who love us.

Accountability is not only a good idea, it's a commandment (1 Peter 5:5). We are told to submit to one another and be clothed with humility. How being accountable works out on a practical level takes us back to goals and action points. You will need to determine to whom you will be submitted, in what areas you will be submitted and when you will communicate to the person(s) to whom you are submitted. Accountability is not to be a fearful experience. Accountability is supposed to be a mutually supportive relationship with another person or small group of people that helps us keep our focus and our faith. By the way, our greatest strength against missing the mark is the power of God within us. 1 John 5:9 tells us, *"No one who is born of God will continue to sin, because he has been born of God."* God's seed on the inside can turn us into lousy sinners on the outside and on the inside! The seed of God in us has taken the wind out of sin's sails! The devil doesn't want you to know this, but it's true. God is committed to your failure at sinning. Godly people, whom you know and love, are also committed to your failure at sinning. That's why we need accountability. Let's face it, even though God has given us "His seed" we all seem to do even better when those we love and who love us are watching.

CONGRATULATIONS!

You've come to the end of your **BBC Manual**.
As you have observed, this isn't just a read-through manual,
it's a workbook, a "tool" to help you develop your walk with God.
I challenge you to "mark up" this manual. Transform it into a gold
mine of nuggets discovered by devotion to the greatest Book by the
greatest Author ever written — the Bible, God's Word to man.

ENDNOTES

1. Robert Flood, <u>America, God Shed His Grace on Thee,</u> Chicago, Moody Press, 1975, p. 29.

2. H. H. Halley, <u>Halley's Bible Handbook,</u> Grand Rapids, Michigan, Zondervan Publishing, 1965, p. 18.

3. Josh McDowell, <u>Evidence That Demands a Verdict</u>, Arrowhead Springs, California, Campus Crusade for Christ, 1972, p. 33.

4. <u>Ten Basic Steps Toward Christian Maturity,</u> Arrowhead Springs, California, Campus Crusade for Christ, September 15, 1968, p. 5.

5. G.F. MacLean, <u>Cambridge Bible for Schools,</u> St. Mark, London, Cambridge University Press, 1893, p. 149.

6. Bernard Ramm, <u>Protestant Christian Evidence</u>, Chicago, Illinois, Moody Press, 1957, p. 170.

7. Henrietta C. Mears, <u>What the Bible is all About</u>, Ventura, California, Regal Books, 1983, p. 19.

8. Josh McDowell, <u>Evidence that Demands a Verdict,</u> Arrowhead Springs, California, Campus Crusade for Christ, 1972, p. 21

9. Sidney Collet, <u>All About the Bible</u>, Old Tappen, New Jersey, Elmery H. Revell Company, n.d., p. 67

10. Nicholas Schaffner, <u>The Beatles Forever</u>, Harrisburg, Pennsylvania, Cameron House, 1977, p. 57

11. McDowell, op. cit., p.23

12. Ramm, op. cit., p. 241.

13. Cleland Boyd McAfee, <u>The Greatest English Classic</u>, New York, New York, Harper and Brothers Publishers, 1912, p.282.

14. Rodden, <u>Student Survival Manual, Vol. 1</u>, Melford, Michigan, Mott Media, 1981, p. 4-4

DEVOTIONAL RESOURCES
TO HELP YOU TURN YOUR BEDROOM
INTO A BIBLE COLLEGE.

The "BEDROOM BIBLE COLLEGE" Manual - This workbook will help you not only read the Bible, it will help you FEED on the Word. Learning the principles of observation, meditation and application will help turn your devotions into delight. Charts and challenges will help you record your progress.

The "WORD ON THE WALL" Poster - Turning your "Bedroom into a Bible College" wouldn't be complete without the "WORD ON THE WALL POSTER." A colorful, contemporary poster complete with over 52 key Bible references listed. The challenge: to memorize and meditate on each of the references. The result will be good success (Joshua 1:8).

The "J12-21 DAY JUMPSTART" Manual – Designed to motivate "tweens" (8-12 year olds) to live the seven words Jesus spoke at the age of 12, this 74 page devotional manual will help jumpstart your son or daughter into a healthy devotional life. Included are 21 true stories of individuals throughout history who were changed around the age of 12. Each day includes an "I MUST" activity along with an opportunity to read and rewrite the Word.

The "J12 GATEWAY GUIDE FOR PARENTS" Manual- This 54 page manual is designed to help parents develop a positive "rite of passage" strategy for their sons and daughters at the strategic ages of 12 and 13. Written by Greg Foley, a father of three, he challenged his boys to turn their Bedrooms into Bible Colleges at the ripe age of 12. This challenge culminated in a J12 ceremony on their 13th birthdays.

For information regarding how to obtain these and other materials contact:

Movement Makers International

PO Box 3940

Broken Arrow, OK 74013-3940

www.j12.com

BOOK STUDY

NAME OF BOOK   DATE

WHO IS THE AUTHOR?   TO WHOM WAS IT WRITTEN?

WHEN WAS IT WRITTEN?   WHERE WAS IT WRITTEN?

WHY WAS THIS BOOK WRITTEN? (DISCOURAGEMENT, CONFLICT, TENSION, ETC)

WHAT IS THE MAIN THEME?   BASIC BOOK OUTLINE (MAIN DIVISIONS
                                          AND SUBDIVISION)

KEY VERSE(S)?

COMMANDS?

PROMISES?

PRINCIPLES (CAUSE AND EFFECT)

BOOK STUDY

NAME OF BOOK

WHO IS THE AUTHOR?

WHEN WAS IT WRITTEN?

WHY WAS THIS BOOK WRITTEN? (DISCOURAGEMENT, CONFLICT, TENSION, ETC)

DATE

TO WHOM WAS IT WRITTEN?

WHERE WAS IT WRITTEN?

WHAT IS THE MAIN THEME?

KEY VERSE(S)?

COMMANDS?

PROMISES?

PRINCIPLES (CAUSE AND EFFECT)

BASIC BOOK OUTLINE (MAIN DIVISIONS AND SUBDIVISION)

BOOK STUDY

NAME OF BOOK   DATE

WHO IS THE AUTHOR?   TO WHOM WAS IT WRITTEN?

WHEN WAS IT WRITTEN?   WHERE WAS IT WRITTEN?

WHY WAS THIS BOOK WRITTEN? (DISCOURAGEMENT, CONFLICT, TENSION, ETC)

WHAT IS THE MAIN THEME?

BASIC BOOK OUTLINE (MAIN DIVISIONS AND SUBDIVISION)

KEY VERSE(S)?

COMMANDS?

PROMISES?

PRINCIPLES (CAUSE AND EFFECT)

TURNING YOUR BEDROOM INTO A BIBLE COLLEGE

BOOK STUDY

NAME OF BOOK   DATE

WHO IS THE AUTHOR?   TO WHOM WAS IT WRITTEN?

WHEN WAS IT WRITTEN?   WHERE WAS IT WRITTEN?

WHY WAS THIS BOOK WRITTEN? (DISCOURAGEMENT, CONFLICT, TENSION, ETC)

WHAT IS THE MAIN THEME?

BASIC BOOK OUTLINE (MAIN DIVISIONS AND SUBDIVISION)

KEY VERSE(S)?

COMMANDS?

PROMISES?

PRINCIPLES (CAUSE AND EFFECT)

BOOK STUDY

NAME OF BOOK   DATE

WHO IS THE AUTHOR?   TO WHOM WAS IT WRITTEN?

WHEN WAS IT WRITTEN?   WHERE WAS IT WRITTEN?

WHY WAS THIS BOOK WRITTEN? (DISCOURAGEMENT, CONFLICT, TENSION, ETC)

WHAT IS THE MAIN THEME?   BASIC BOOK OUTLINE (MAIN DIVISIONS
                                     AND SUBDIVISION)

KEY VERSE(S)?

COMMANDS?

PROMISES?

PRINCIPLES (CAUSE AND EFFECT)

CHAPTER STUDY

CHAPTER

MAIN MESSAGE

MAIN CHARACTERS

KEY VERSES

DATE

BBC
MANUAL

KEY VERSE(S)?

COMMANDS?

PROMISES?

PRINCIPLES

BASIC BOOK OUTLINE (MAIN DIVISIONS AND SUBDIVISION)

CHAPTER

DATE

MAIN MESSAGE

MAIN CHARACTERS

KEY VERSES

KEY VERSE(S)?

BASIC BOOK OUTLINE (MAIN DIVISIONS
AND SUBDIVISION)

COMMANDS?

PROMISES?

PRINCIPLES

TURNING YOUR
BEDROOM
INTO A BIBLE
COLLEGE

CHAPTER

MAIN MESSAGE

MAIN CHARACTERS

KEY VERSES

DATE

KEY VERSE(S)?

COMMANDS?

PROMISES?

PRINCIPLES

BASIC BOOK OUTLINE (MAIN DIVISIONS AND SUBDIVISION)

CHAPTER   DATE
MAIN MESSAGE

MAIN CHARACTERS

KEY VERSES

KEY VERSE(S)?   BASIC BOOK OUTLINE (MAIN DIVISIONS
                                AND SUBDIVISION)

COMMANDS?

PROMISES?

PRINCIPLES

VERSE REFERENCE   DATE

WRITE OUT THE VERSE, USING A SEPARATE LINE FOR EACH DIVISION
OF THOUGHT: (CLUE- DIVISIONS OF THOUGHT OFTEN COME AFTER
CONNECTIVE WORDS SUCH AS: AND, BECAUSE, FOR, IF, AND, THEREFORE).

KEY WORD(S) - THEIR MEANING?

COMMANDS?

PROMISES?

PRINCIPLES (CAUSE AND EFFECT RELATIONSHIPS)?

WHAT DOES THIS VERSE MEAN TO ME?

VERSE STUDY

VERSE REFERENCE   **DATE**

WRITE OUT THE VERSE, USING A SEPARATE LINE FOR EACH DIVISION
OF THOUGHT: (CLUE– DIVISIONS OF THOUGHT OFTEN COME AFTER
CONNECTIVE WORDS SUCH AS: AND, BECAUSE, FOR, IF, AND, THEREFORE).

KEY WORD(S) - THEIR MEANING?

COMMANDS?

PROMISES?

PRINCIPLES (CAUSE AND EFFECT RELATIONSHIPS)?

WHAT DOES THIS VERSE MEAN TO ME?

TURNING YOUR
BEDROOM
INTO A BIBLE
COLLEGE

VERSE STUDY

VERSE REFERENCE   DATE

WRITE OUT THE VERSE, USING A SEPARATE LINE FOR EACH DIVISION
OF THOUGHT: (CLUE► DIVISIONS OF THOUGHT OFTEN COME AFTER
CONNECTIVE WORDS SUCH AS: AND, BECAUSE, FOR, IF, AND, THEREFORE).

KEY WORD(S) - THEIR MEANING?

COMMANDS?

PROMISES?

PRINCIPLES (CAUSE AND EFFECT RELATIONSHIPS)?

WHAT DOES THIS VERSE MEAN TO ME?

VERSE REFERENCE   DATE

WRITE OUT THE VERSE, USING A SEPARATE LINE FOR EACH DIVISION
OF THOUGHT: (CLUE- DIVISIONS OF THOUGHT OFTEN COME AFTER
CONNECTIVE WORDS SUCH AS: AND, BECAUSE, FOR, IF, AND, THEREFORE).

KEY WORD(S) - THEIR MEANING?

COMMANDS?

PROMISES?

PRINCIPLES (CAUSE AND EFFECT RELATIONSHIPS)?

WHAT DOES THIS VERSE MEAN TO ME?

BIBLE CHARACTER

REFERENCES

DATE

DESCRIBE THEIR CHILDHOOD EXPERIENCES.

DESCRIBE GOD'S CALL ON THEIR LIFE.

DESCRIBE THEIR RESPONSE TO GOD'S CALL ON THEIR LIFE (POSITIVE AND/OR NEGATIVE).

OUTLINE THEIR LIFE IN STAGES/SIGNIFICANT TURNING POINTS.

WHAT LESSONS CAN YOU DRAW FOR YOUR LIFE FROM THEIR LIFE?

BIBLE CHARACTER

REFERENCES

DATE

BIBLE CHARACTER   DATE
REFERENCES

DESCRIBE THEIR CHILDHOOD EXPERIENCES.

DESCRIBE GOD'S CALL ON THEIR LIFE.

DESCRIBE THEIR RESPONSE TO GOD'S CALL ON THEIR LIFE (POSITIVE AND/OR NEGATIVE).

OUTLINE THEIR LIFE IN STAGES/SIGNIFICANT TURNING POINTS.

WHAT LESSONS CAN YOU DRAW FOR YOUR LIFE FROM THEIR LIFE?

BIBLE CHARACTER

REFERENCES

DATE

DESCRIBE THEIR CHILDHOOD EXPERIENCES.

DESCRIBE GOD'S CALL ON THEIR LIFE.

DESCRIBE THEIR RESPONSE TO GOD'S CALL ON THEIR LIFE (POSITIVE AND/OR NEGATIVE).

OUTLINE THEIR LIFE IN STAGES/SIGNIFICANT TURNING POINTS.

WHAT LESSONS CAN YOU DRAW FOR YOUR LIFE FROM THEIR LIFE?

BIBLE CHARACTER

DATE

CHARACTER STUDY

BIBLE CHARACTER   DATE
REFERENCES

DESCRIBE THEIR CHILDHOOD EXPERIENCES.

DESCRIBE GOD'S CALL ON THEIR LIFE.

DESCRIBE THEIR RESPONSE TO GOD'S CALL ON THEIR LIFE (POSITIVE AND/OR NEGATIVE).

OUTLINE THEIR LIFE IN STAGES/SIGNIFICANT TURNING POINTS.

WHAT LESSONS CAN YOU DRAW FOR YOUR LIFE FROM THEIR LIFE?

TOPICAL STUDY

TOPIC	DATE

KEY REFERENCES	OBSERVATIONS / INSIGHTS / OUTLINES

WHAT HAVE I LEARNED?

TOPICAL STUDY

TOPIC   DATE

KEY REFERENCES

OBSERVATIONS / INSIGHTS / OUTLINES

WHAT HAVE I LEARNED?

TURNING YOUR
BEDROOM
INTO A BIBLE
COLLEGE

TOPICAL STUDY

TOPIC

DATE

KEY REFERENCES

OBSERVATIONS / INSIGHTS / OUTLINES

WHAT HAVE I LEARNED?

TOPICAL STUDY

TOPIC	DATE

KEY REFERENCES	OBSERVATIONS / INSIGHTS / OUTLINES

WHAT HAVE I LEARNED?

TURNING YOUR BEDROOM INTO A BIBLE COLLEGE

THE
BBC
MANUAL

TURNING YOUR
BEDROOM
INTO A BIBLE
COLLEGE

TURNING YOUR BEDROOM INTO A BIBLE COLLEGE

TURNING YOUR
BEDROOM
INTO A BIBLE
COLLEGE